RIP OFF YOUR BLINDFOLD

Also by Dr. Dele Ola

Be a Change Agent:
Leadership in a Time of Exponential Change

Pursuit of Personal Leadership: Practical Principles of Personal Achievement

RIP OFF YOUR BLINDFOLD

SEE HOW SUCCESSFUL PEOPLE SEE

Dr. Dele Ola

The Prowezz Company

Published by The Prowezz Company, Inc.
Email: theprowezzcompany@gmail.com

Edited by Bobbi Beatty of Silver Scroll Services, Calgary, Alberta

Rip Off Your Blindfold / Dr. Dele Ola
First Edition 2023

ISBN
978-1-7779645-6-6 (paperback)
978-1-7779645-7-3 (e-book)

1. *PSYCHOLOGY / Creative Ability*
2. *SELF-HELP / Motivational & Inspirational*
3. *BUSINESS & ECONOMICS / Leadership*

This book may be purchased in bulk at quantity discounts for corporate, educational, reselling, gifting, or promotional purposes through the author. Kindly visit www.deleola.com or call 1 (204) 421-4018 for more information.

DEDICATION

To those who are on a journey of self-discovery, who are pursuing personal excellence.

Contents

Seeing Clearly Is Not What You Might Think It Is

My family had an unexpected experience in December 2019. We had planned to spend a few days shopping in Fargo, North Dakota, before the new year. It was in the dead cold of winter, the day after Boxing Day, that we set out on the highway for our three-and-a-half-hour journey south. This wasn't a new adventure for us as we had embarked on the same trip at the same time of year many years in a row. The weather was fair in Winnipeg, only about -5°C with a relatively cloudless sky. There was, however, a bit of windchill caused by wind gusts somewhere around 35 km/hour, and a few snowflakes were drifting across the highway as a result. Nevertheless, it was not weather we had not experienced many times before. We were so comfortable with the conditions that we didn't even bother to check the weather forecast for Fargo. That was our fatal error.

Shortly after crossing the Canada-US border at Emerson, we saw a thick cloud ahead. We didn't think it was anything serious until we drove right into it. It was the densest fog I had ever seen in my entire life. I had seen thick fog in the city in the past, which always made it difficult to drive with the low visibility, but all the fog I'd experienced before couldn't compare to this time. Within about ten minutes, we were right in the middle of the fog with zero visibility. It became difficult to keep going, yet turning back was also hard. The situation was complicated by snowdrifts and crosswinds. We were in the middle of both a dense fog and a snowstorm. Driving became arduous and terrifying. Parking on the shoulder to wait for the weather to clear out would also have been a bad option as other vehicles could run into us. So, there we were, driving with zero visibility and not knowing how long the weather would last. Even taking an offramp was a risk as there were heavy piles of snow on the roads branching off the highway. What were we to do?

The lack of an ability to see clearly slowed our journey. Progress was difficult without visibility. We lost speed. We were in danger. Would we make it to Fargo? We were on the road for much longer than needed, risking our lives and losing our excitement of the road trip while trying to just make it to Fargo alive. In the end, we decided to keep driving, but slowly, despite the extreme weather conditions. It took many additional hours of risk and guesswork to push through until we arrived in Fargo. The highway was eventually closed shortly after we arrived.

My family was fortunate to have reached our destination in the soupy fog, but we knew many others did not. While still on the road, we came across many vehicles already in the ditch. We saw lots of accidents on the way, with some vehicles even turned on their sides and others stuck in the snow drifts. The weather had dealt a blow to many truck drivers too, whose trucks had also rolled over. What turned out to be a three-day snowstorm wreaked havoc over the city. Our family was stranded in our hotel room for days as the whole city of Fargo was locked down due to the heavy snowstorm and foggy weather. What should have been a day trip turned into an extended stay in a dreary hotel room.

Have you ever tried to drive in heavy fog? Well, most people do—every day. A vast number of the world's almost eight billion people, perhaps 80 to 90 percent, drive through an internal fog every day as if they're blindfolded. After years of observation, dissection, and analysis, I've determined that this blindfold is the reason we have a serious abuse of authority and power in corporations and politics. It is why society does not function optimally, the reason there is dysfunctional leadership at all levels. Many people are given authority over others through power, money, or deception but cannot see the true essence of the very authority they have been given. The dense fog of the inner blindfold they wear obscures their vision. They make decisions without the discipline of clear-sightedness. This blindfold is even responsible for the lack of success many people experience in their personal and professional lives. Most people just keep driving on, day after day, without a full view of the road or the landscape around them. They coast on in mental obscurity, making personal and business decisions without clear-sightedness. What a misadventure!

Over many years, I've watched people go through their careers and personal lives with such difficulty—and I've come to see why. We tend to see the world with our *eyesight*, seeing it only through the lens of our personal experience, interpreting life through the spyglass of our limited understanding and allowing our individual interpretations to becloud our judgment. Many people find it hard—if not impossible—to see beyond what they can see. It's like there's a kind of blindfold that covers most people's eyes. In fact, I'm quite sure most people aren't even aware they're wearing a blindfold, even the smartest and most educated of us.

When you look at the world, what do you see? Hmm … let me ask that question more correctly. When you look at the world, *how* do you see? What you see is a function of your *eyesight*, whereas how you see is a function of your *insight*. Going through life without clear-sightedness of the mind is like driving through the fog. Leading people without clear-sightedness is like leading a tribe through a zero-visibility snowstorm. Running a business, an organization, a family, or society without clear-sightedness is like navigating through pea-soup fog with no option of stopping, pulling over, or changing direction. It amazes me every time I see people just continue driving ahead at full speed, deeper and deeper into the fog, even though they cannot see clearly. Somehow, they don't seem to feel the danger, the risk, as they zoom through their fog with no thought for the safety of themselves or others. What a catastrophe!

What you see is a function of your eyesight, whereas how you see is a function of your insight.

Do you feel like you lack complete clarity when making decisions at work, in your business, at home, or in your personal affairs? Does it seem like you are coasting onward but sometimes guessing your way through major life experiences? Do you feel like you do not always have the answer? You are not alone. Most of us do not always have the answer. Yet it is still our responsibility to see clearly to avoid major pitfalls, for ourselves and others.

Again, *what* we see outwardly is a function of our eyes. It's called eyesight. *How* we see though is a function of the eyes of our minds. It's called insight. We must start seeing clearly through the lens of our minds. We must acquire the clear-sightedness needed for success in various aspects of our lives. Successful people, leaders, those who make great strides in their lives, those who leave a mark in the world and become notable, those who have personal fulfillment, and those who change the world for the better see with their insight rather than their eyesight. The mind sees much more, and much farther, than the eyes can see. You can see the world clearly through your mind without eyesight, but you cannot see the world clearly through your eyes without insight. Anyone who does not see clearly with their mind is driving through fog.

What do I mean by that? The concept is still vague, I know. Let me explain with a story that shows that it is not *what* people see that holds them back, it is *how* they see.

Let's discuss Erik Weihenmayer, a renowned mountain climber, adventurer, and speaker.[1] Erik was diagnosed with retinoschisis as a child and started losing his physical vision in his early teenage years, but he rejected the idea of being sidelined because of physical blindness. So, as a wrestler in high school, he made it to the National Junior Freestyle Wrestling Championship in Iowa, representing his home state of Connecticut.

Thereafter, Erik graduated with a double major in English and communications from Boston College and became a middle-school teacher and wrestling coach at Phoenix Country Day School. As the years passed, he became passionate about rock climbing, having discovered his natural ability to tactically scan rocks with his hands and feet for a hold. In 1995, he began a quest to conquer the world's most formidable mountains after reaching the highest point in North America: Denali, as it is known as in the native Inuit language. Erik eventually became the first physically blind person to conquer Mount Everest, a feat he achieved on May 25, 2001, and the details of which were published in his honor in a *Time Magazine* cover story. He later conquered the Seven Summits—the highest point on every continent—and climbed Puncak Jaya (Glorious Peak), or Carstensz Pyramid, on the island of Papua New Guinea. With his indefatigable spirit of adventure, Erik, in 2014, even kayaked the entire 277 miles of the Colorado River through the Grand Canyon.

The story of Erik Weihenmayer teaches us that one's true experiences are not so much about what they can see with their eyesight but about how much they can see with their insight. Blindness is not only defined as having less than 10 percent normal vision in the more efficient physical eye, but it is also defined as the inability to discern or judge, having no regard for rational discrimination, guidance, or restriction, and doing things without the knowledge of facts that could serve as guidance or cause bias.[2] Therefore, the true definition of blindness is a lack of insight, perception, or judgment. Humankind's greatest flaw is to be possessed of physical sight but lack clear-sightedness of the mind, to be devoid of the ability to see the world clearly through a lens of sound principles and intuitive understanding. We must become open-minded, learn compassion, show empathy, and determine to make a difference.

I wrote this book to help you learn how successful people see. I aim to help remove the barriers to clear-sightedness, the dense fog that prevents people from effectively leading, running successful businesses, accomplishing great things, reaching personal goals, and fulfilling their personal visions. I intend to ignite your curiosity and provoke you to use clear-sightedness in life and leadership. So throughout, I'll use thought-provoking personal stories, true stories from research, and fictional stories to highlight the central message of this book: how to see the world clearly through a new lens. Each chapter is a piece of literature that may stand alone yet is interconnected to the other chapters in principle. I hope you enjoy the stories while picking up invaluable lessons as you navigate each chapter. Let us begin the journey.

Humankind's greatest flaw is to be possessed of physical sight but lack clear-sightedness of the mind, to be devoid of the ability to see the world clearly through a lens of sound principles and intuitive understanding.

CHAPTER 1

Changing Your Mental View

Early evenings are usually momentous in the Dwumati Forest in the open woodlands of the mystical Awalaffe Kingdom, the kingdom of the animals. Dwumati is home to huge herds of wild animals, including hippos, buffalo, gazelles, giraffes, zebras, elephants, and all their wild-cat predators.

It was a breezy night, a few hours after the scorching sunshine had abated and the atmosphere was graced by the northern winds that made the trees dance with their rustling leaves. Birds chirped and twittered as they rested on the waltzing branches. That evening in Dwumati was no different from many others until a terrified herd of buffalo stampeded eastward in a confused manner. Some ran unchecked but others just dragged their feet as if utterly dumbfounded by what had just happened.

Incidentally, the news correspondent for the *Awalaffe Animal News* arrived at the scene just in time to cover the story. She started interviewing the onlookers and eyewitnesses, and the first animal available was a buffalo, who was still fidgety and frightened after escaping what he described as a gruesome killing by a female lion. According to the buffalo, one of his siblings had just been hunted down and murdered in a bloody massacre after what had felt like a ten-minute brawl between the herd and the pride of lions.

"Our forest is a lush land filled with exuberance and an abundance of pasture for our family to graze. We live in harmony with many other animal families. However, the lions are a family of bullies, scoundrels that cause mayhem throughout the land," explained the buffalo. "We have lived in terror from generation to generation, and there has been no salvation for us. Now we have just lost one of our most stately members, my own brother, in a most horrifying manner. He was killed in cold blood by the merciless female lion, only to become food for her cubs. We buffalo are hunted the most by wild cats and crocodiles in this forest," the buffalo lamented.

A hefty male lion and a fierce-looking female lion standing nearby listened intently as the buffalo told his story. When the buffalo sensed the two lions were about to approach him, he said no more and turned slowly around to join his demoralized family. So the news correspondent turned to the female lion and asked her to describe the incident.

"We have gone five nights in a row without food for our cubs," the lion said. "We have lost twenty-five cubs to death by starvation in the last year, alongside some of their mothers. We are so happy to now have one of the biggest buffalo for dinner for some of the little ones. But as you can see, the meat is barely enough for them. Most of the other animals in the forest—the zebras, buffalo, elephants, and monkeys—have their food ready-made for them by nature. They can just come out to graze or pluck from trees. We must struggle to find food. No one gives freely to us, not even nature, and sometimes we even lose our kills to hyena theft. As the family that lacks the most in the jungle, we are now on a hunting spree so we can preserve our young and defend our livelihood," explained the female lion.

To the north of the crime scene was a swampy area slightly flooded by run-offs from the rain that had fallen earlier in the day. The swamp was next to the Awalaffe River where the slender-snouted crocodiles live. The news correspondent decided to try and get an interview from one of the crocodiles to try and corroborate what had been reported by others. However, the crocodiles declined to offer their perspectives. They couldn't care less about what anyone thought or felt about the incident.

Now back to our world. Let me ask you this: did you take a side? Did you find yourself empathizing with the buffalo or the lion? Chances are choosing a side came automatically, without you even meaning to.

Based on the different perspectives of the buffalo and the female lion, which side of the story do you agree with? Do you feel more sympathy for the buffalo who had just lost his brother to a gruesome murder, or do you feel sorry for the young lions who die daily because of food deprivation? Or neither?

You may conclude that there are two different sides to the same story. You may be the buffalo, or you may be the lion.

Everyone sees from their own perspective and experience, from their own frame of reference. Take some time to think about that. Are you the buffalo or the lion? Or are you the crocodile? Or are you perhaps another species who simply sees the merit in both points of view?

There Are Only Two People in the World

When you saw what this section was titled, what did you think? That I made an error? You may think I'm off my rocker, but yes, there are only two people in the world: you and others. For example, in a family, there is you and there are the others in your family: this might include your siblings, parents, children, and/or spouse. In the workplace, there is you and there are the others in your workplace: your employer and colleagues and customers. In politics, there is you and there are the others in the political sphere, where they are the public, parliamentarians or congressmen, and/or your party.

As humans, we tend to see things primarily from our own perspectives as dictated by our own needs, experiences, and personal preferences. We generally see all others as the other side of the equation. Our perspectives tend to be biased toward our own needs and dominate our immediate responses unless we can learn to see differently. Meanwhile, thinking beyond our own needs to alter our perspectives is not automatic. It takes awareness. It takes work.

The reason we're blindfolded is simple: the human mind first learned self-centeredness in childhood before learning to become selfless in later years. We were all born as a little helpless baby. Our parents and families gave us everything we needed. As an infant, you just cried when you needed something, and there it was. That behavior continued when you were a toddler. You made demands and got your way. At that age, the whole universe revolved around you. And then self-awareness set in when you discovered you in the mirror. Of course you were the center of the universe before then. You didn't know any differently.

We spend the most formative years of our lives learning self-centeredness, but then we start working to reverse that order as we grow older. No wonder it is difficult to get people to naturally see from other peoples' perspectives. We were all born with a natural tendency to be selfish. I remember John C. Maxwell, author of *Developing the Leader Within You 2.0*, citing an example in a speech, and he asked the audience who they first looked for in a group photo. The answer was you, of course. If you take a photo with a group of friends or your family, it is natural for you to quickly look for yourself first when you see the photo. Sometimes you might even look at the photo, make comments about your appearance alone, then forget to check out the other people in the same photo. It's all about you. You care much less about how others appear in the same photo. But don't feel bad. We've all done it because we're hardwired to.

The human mind first learned self-centeredness in childhood before learning to become selfless in later years.

Nevertheless, our ability to become conscious of others and then see from their perspectives through our intuitive understanding is critical to our success in life. Becoming conscious of others requires deliberate action—and practice. "When we get too caught up in the busyness of the world, we lose connection with one another—and ourselves," said Jack Kornfield, one of the world's leading mindfulness-meditation experts.

Although our world, for selfish reasons, may seem like the jungle where the lion must hunt others down for survival while the buffalo must take cover to stay alive, the survival-of-the-fittest mentality does not take people and society far. It may seem as though that's just the way it is, the way it must be. But consider how all of society could flourish if we stepped out of ourselves and looked at the world as others do. Does it have to be dog-eat-dog or survival-of-the-fittest? If we all took off our blindfolds and used our insight, could we not all thrive?

But you ask, is life not competitive? Do we not have to compete with others to improve our circumstances—or even survive in some cases? Of course, we know that life is competitive. However, the competition of life is not about consuming others just to create fat around our middles. It is not about stepping on others to climb higher up the ladder. It is not about trampling on others to succeed in life. Those who live the jungle life for empty reasons cause more problems than they solve. They are blind. In a peaceful meadow where people thrive and make strides together, you'll find those who have insight and an intuitive understanding of the needs of others. This helps everyone solve problems and move ahead, unlike most of humankind, who live in the jungle. That is the real competition: self-competition, pushing your personal boundaries to do something spectacular in the world and for the world.

When we cannot see from other people's perspectives, we cannot help them solve problems. It is only when we start shifting our sight away from our own needs to the needs of others that we begin to gain insight into solving shared problems. In turn, solving problems and addressing the challenges faced by others is one of the biggest ways we make headway in life. Most people are unable to raise themselves out of mediocrity because of self-centeredness. Everything is about their own needs and survival, their own perspectives on life. People who cannot see from other people's perspectives lack clear-sightedness. They are driving through the fog.

Let us look at it in more practical terms. In fact, let us look at an example.

The Man Who Saw the Autobody Workers Clearly

I came across a 2007 publication by the American Chemical Society.[1] It was the story of the remarkable person behind the discovery of Scotch® Transparent Tape, the same astounding product found in every home, office, and school today. This tape, described as the most ubiquitous and successful product ever developed, was first manufactured by Minnesota Mining and Manufacturing (3M).

Richard Drew worked for 3M during the 1920s when the autobody workers and their customers became obsessed with dual-toned colors on cars. It was no small job to put two colors on cars and do it well. Workers needed to mask off portions of the car body while other portions were being painted, yet no one really knew how to do the job well. The workers improvised by gluing old newspapers to the body and windows using paste, homemade glue, and adhesive tape to create sharp demarcations at the boundary between two colors. What was the result? In many cases, the adhesives bonded to the body such that when removed, they ruined the paint job. It was a real headache.

It was during that era that the twenty-three-year-old Drew, working in sales at 3M, was taking samples of their waterproof sandpaper to neighboring autobody shops for testing. One morning in 1923, Drew walked into one of the shops to find a disgruntled worker lamenting the ruination of yet another paint job. Drew had seen this happen on many occasions on his previous visits, but this time around, he decided to speak up, to express what was on his mind. He was tired of seeing the frustration again and again and wanted to find a way to solve the problem.

"I can produce a tape that will end a painter's torment," he declared.

He made that pledge based on his willingness to help solve a problem. However, his minimal education—he was an engineering-school dropout—experience, and know-how did not match his optimism. He was audacious with his promise but had no idea what he was getting himself into.

Although Drew did not seem like an innovator, he garnered the support of his superiors at 3M, who were looking for ways to diversify the company's product lines. Thus began Drew's journey to figure out how to deliver on the bold promise he'd made on impulse. He started with the adhesive used in 3M's waterproof sandpaper and spent the next two years experimenting with vegetable oils, resins, linseed, chicle, and glue glycerin. He eventually successfully developed the first Scotch® Masking Tape, a formula containing a grade of cabinetmaker's glue and glycerin on treated crepe-paper backing. This spectacular product adhered strongly on the car's body yet stripped off easily without ruining the paint job. It eventually became the first in the line of Scotch® brand tapes.

In 1929, just four years after the introduction of the Scotch® Masking Tape, Drew attempted a new challenge. A St. Paul, Minnesota, insulation firm, Flaxlinum Company, had been contracted to insulate hundreds of refrigerated railroad cars. The challenge was that the company needed to put moisture-proof wrappings around the batts to be used in the refrigerated cars. Drew and his team at 3M, starting with the Scotch® Masking Tape, took on the challenge, but their effort proved futile as nothing was sufficiently watertight for the application.

Though that venture failed, it would lead to the answer to a later problem. Not long after his failure, a 3M employee showed Drew a sample of DuPont's new cellophane, a material being considered for packaging at 3M. He immediately saw the potential for cellophane to become Flaxlinum's backing material, and after several experiments, found what he believed was the solution to the problem. By that time though, Flaxlinum had lost interest. Undeterred, Drew and his team turned to the food industry, which was already using cellophane for wrapping food but needed to find a way to seal their packaging. It was no small feat for 3M to produce something that worked for the food industry. It took several months of overcoming the innovation challenges, but eventually, Drew and his team finally invented Scotch® Cellulose Tape, which was later renamed Scotch® Transparent Tape, a magical household material that has been made into several variants to solve our daily problems ever since. It's still one of the leading adhesive tapes in the world today.

It took Richard Drew, with his keen and genuine interest in solving other people's problems, to invent the tapes. He observed the frustration of the autobody workers, gained insight into their needs, and put everything he had into finding a solution. His audacious desire to help others drove him to making the transparent tape, which is still being used by us all today. Until his death in 1980 at the age of eighty-one, Drew continued to find better versions of the tapes he'd invented and created breakthrough adhesives for many industries. He was inducted to the National Inventors Hall of Fame in 2007.

As I stated earlier, there are only two people in the world: you and others. Clearly seeing others and recognizing their perspectives is an important key that allows us to unlock our own advancements in life. I remember the words of Pastor Mike Murdock, who once said, "Your rewards in life are determined by the kinds of problems you are willing to solve for someone." Nevertheless, we cannot solve any problem for anyone until we begin to see others clearly, until we begin to see them with our insight and intuitive understanding of their needs and challenges. We must rip off our blindfolds and cure our blindness.

We cannot solve any problem for anyone until we begin to see others clearly, until we begin to see them with our insight and intuitive understanding of their needs and challenges.

So then, let us examine some ways you can cure your blindness and practice seeing others clearly.

See Them Clearly

When you see others, how do you see? No, I didn't say that wrong. I didn't mean to ask, "When you look at someone, what do you see?" I want you to think about *how* you see. Renowned author Laura Ingalls Wilder said, "Persons appear to us according to the light we throw upon them from our own minds." What light do you throw upon other people? To see others clearly, to cure your blindness, you must be willing to do the work. Embracing the necessary values means shedding your own perspectives and demonstrating your intuitive understanding of others, signifying a sense of perception and clear judgment. Here are the steps you can practice on your journey to seeing others with your insight rather than your eyesight.

1. Bestow respect and be gracious

Respect is a word used too commonly in the business world, such that we could say it has lost its meaning. Most organizations even list respect as part of their core values. The word is so abused in corporations that it has become commonplace. Who even needs to label "respect" as a core value for an organization? Is respect not a personal virtue that should be engrained in every one of us? If an organization does not value respect without it having to be stated, then something must be wrong somewhere.

People in management positions and positions of authority shout their pedestrian core value—respect—from the rooftop without insight into what it really means to respect others. They ask their employees—and many times without practicing it themselves—to practice a commonplace value that only has rhetorical significance without properly defining what it means to respect others.

What about the meaning of respect in society? Do those who run our governments respect their citizens? Why do some politicians say one thing and then do otherwise? If those who make decisions for the rest of society do not really understand the needs of the people they govern, and never make the appropriate effort to gain insight into the people's needs, then we should ask if those politicians truly respect the people.

As obvious as the importance of respect seems to be, it is still lacking in many individuals due to a lack of clear-sightedness. Respect is a personal value deeply rooted in the willingness to acknowledge the personality, idea, or disposition of others. It is a value expressed by those who see others clearly with their insight. Respect is demonstrated by those who see others the way they really are, the way they could be, and what they need.

There is no excuse for disrespecting people. Someone may hide behind the saying that "You are addressed the way you are dressed." Those who address or treat people disrespectfully because of outer appearances are small-minded and lack insight. The self-worth of an individual is not proportional to their manner of dress, the cost of their necklace, the make of their car, or the elegance of their look. Those who are respectable do not need to adorn themselves with jewelry or expensive apparel to earn respect. Think back on your own life. Have you ever seen someone apologize after treating another person disrespectfully, and the person apologizing cites their lack of awareness of who the other person was or what their social status was at the time of the encounter? That is a lack of insight.

Those who have taken it upon themselves to respect others possess intuitive understanding. Respecting other people is a way of buying goodwill for ourselves. Respect begets respect. We do not achieve great things in isolation from other people. When those around you feel genuinely valued and respected by you, you will earn their goodwill to support whatever great thing you are working to achieve. More importantly, if you are insightful enough to truly respect people, it will be easy to spot opportunities to meet their needs.

You and I can learn to respect others in many ways. First, start seeing other people through the lens of who they have the potential to become, and do that upfront. In fact, it is much safer to think that everyone you encounter is important—because they really are. It takes someone with insight to see another person beyond what the eyes can see. Respect for others comes organically and easily when we consistently look for the potential good in them rather than making assumptions about them.

Second, and this can take practice, learn to believe in others' abilities and accept what they produce. This is important in teams working together to achieve an objective. As humans, we develop varying degrees of intellectual and physical capabilities as we grow and learn, and everyone produces based on what they are capable of at any one time. We must learn to genuinely accept others' output, even when we recognize room for improvement. They too will continue to learn and grow and will learn from their current situation.

Third, take notice of others' effort. When we see people clearly, we recognize their contributions, giving us an opportunity to praise and honor them. You might say, "But I do recognize others' efforts." But ask yourself how regularly you notice though. And further, how regularly do you acknowledge their efforts? Do those working with you know their work means something to you? How often do you notice what others do well? When last did you give kudos to someone? Are you clear-sighted enough to see the good works performed by those who help you achieve your goals? You may be surprised to discover how much of others' efforts slips by unnoticed while you're preoccupied with your own efforts.

Last, if by regularly practicing the previous steps you come to truly respect those you work with and live with, you will come to acknowledge how much their efforts affect yours. So let others know how important they and their efforts are every time the opportunity presents itself. People who feel respected are usually motivated to keep up the good work. It is important to see others clearly with insight and respect them accordingly.

2. Remove bias and obliterate prejudice

At this point in time, we should ideally be able to say, "Gone are the days when religious, racial, gender, or any other form of bias exists." However, we need to ask ourselves if we have removed biases and obliterated prejudices. Have we really made progress, or we have continued promoting systemic biases? I do not know the answer, but I am aware that there are still plenty of biases in the world, and there are thoughts and beliefs individuals hold on to at the disadvantage of others.

These biases are not limited to any one culture but run through most cultures. Whatever those prejudices may be, they too are blindfolds. It takes someone with clear sight, someone who possesses intuitive understanding, to see beyond the racial, ethnic, religious, gender, economic, geographic, and political divides. As humans, our commonalities are whopping compared to our differences. Unfortunately, those who operate within the obscurity of their bias blindfold continue to major in the minor; in other words, their words and actions are perpetually driven by their bias despite these

As humans, our commonalities are whopping compared to our differences.

people numbering only a minority of the population. They place their prejudice before objective reasoning and work to achieve their own needs rather than the needs of others.

Let me give you a typical but subtle example. Some people are more comfortable working with, or giving opportunities to, people of the same racial or tribal background, and sometimes from only their own family or friends. That nepotism becomes a blindfold that prevents clear judgment and affects one's ability to deal fairly with others who don't fit in their personal bias category. In most cases, nepotism does not regard competence and accountability but places biases above aptitude, expertise, or merit.

Once upon a time, back when the world was a more closed, segregated place with less immigration, travel, and news coverage, it was common to work with only people like you. It was all you knew. Now that the world is smaller and more connected and aware than ever before, it's a poor excuse for one to say they have never really worked with anyone from a particular group before so they're not sure how things will turn out. It's an excuse founded on paranoia and fear of the unknown. This delusion may be the reason you find many modern-day organizations, for example in North America, with almost zero diversity in their workforce despite their fairly large size. It is a blindfold, an obstruction to clear-sightedness.

In the twenty-first century business climate, if you are an entrepreneur, a business owner, a corporate leader, a religious leader, or a leader of any sort, having an open mind to diversity and being intentional in hunting for the right skills, talents, and competence irrespective of people's background characteristics is important to your success. According to an article published in Forbes, if the United States blocked refugees and immigrants from coming into the country, more than half of the billion-dollar start-up companies would be lost.[2] The writer of the article, Stuart Anderson, explained that fifty of the ninety-one start-up companies in the United States valued at over $1 billion as of October 1, 2018, not publicly traded on the stock market had at least one immigrant founder.

Everyone serious about making progress in today's business climate must remove the biases and obliterate prejudice. The same holds true for both personal lives and politics. The world has indeed become exceptionally more diversified with massive global talent mobility. Some insightful and clear-sighted people will take advantage of the opportunity to advance their cause while those who remain blindfolded will continue to grapple with the truth and wonder why they seem to have to shout louder and push harder to achieve the same success as those who removed their blindfolds and now use their insight.

I also can't help but question if various governments' quota systems and introduction of equity, diversity, and inclusiveness programs is the real solution. Bias and prejudice will continue until people change their minds, the attitudes of their minds, and become clear-sighted. The main problem is that of short-sightedness, the blindness of the mind. Many people continue to be unaware of their blindfolds, and some who are aware of them choose to keep them on. Most people do not see with insight. One must strive to see beyond one's own limited scope of understanding and remove bias from one's mind before the world can evolve and accept people as people. Simply making policies without dealing with the root of the problem won't clear people's sight.

I was among a group of people discussing how to support newcomers to Canada a while ago. I was about the only member of a visible minority group in the discussion. A major item on the discussion list was the needs of newcomers and immigrants in the community. The attendees concluded that what most newcomers needed was language training and education. I sat there unsurprised as usual as I had been in several other meetings where the challenges of equity, diversity, and inclusiveness had been discussed. This group of societal majorities, looking through a narrow lens and maybe a misinformed perspective, made lots of assumptions on what the immigrants needed without truly reaching the nucleus of the issues of the people they were sincerely hoping to serve.

One must strive to see beyond one's own limited scope of understanding and remove bias from their mind before the world can evolve and accept people as people.

How did I understand what the newcomers needed? Well, I was once the newcomer and I remembered what I needed most to integrate into society. While many people from diverse geographic backgrounds might have needed language training, I hadn't; I could thankfully read, write, and communicate in English exceptionally well compared to most immigrants. I could avail myself of additional education as I did, but my previous education was sufficient to work wherever my skill was needed. For someone like me, generalizing that what I needed was language training and education would have been a blunder, a common one-size-fits-all error.

So, what did I need, or rather not need, for my career? I did not need anyone to look at my university degree and wonder if I was as educated as them just because I came from Africa. I did not want anyone to ask if I could speak or write English properly just because of my color. I did not want a potential employer to screen out my resume from the pool of applicants just because of my non-English name or because they had never worked with an African and were unsure how I would behave or "fit in."

All I needed was an opportunity, to be given a chance to compete fairly with other job applicants without racial prejudice or any other form of discrimination. I wanted a merit-based system that just placed me on the same playing field as others, a system that would treat me like the human being I am without thinking I did not belong. Do you also think we need a system like that? Of course, you do, or you wouldn't still be reading this book. That which has necessitated deliberate actions by governments to intervene in issues of diversity is the blindness of the mind, and it must be cured.

And let me clarify that diversity doesn't just include social differences such as race, ethnicity, color, language, religion, and the like. We also need diversity of opinions, ideas, and models. We need people that see the world differently but clearly. No one has a monopoly on ideas.

Most biases are just a form of stereotype and lack of clear-sightedness. Most people aren't even aware they have a blindfold wrapped tightly around their inner eyes. Many organizations have missed out on adding potentially great people to their teams because of stereotyping. Instead, they've built a team of people homogeneous in background and thinking. As such, opportunities have eluded many people and organizations because of the lack of insight into the advantages that diversity brings. By the same token, we do a great disservice to the talented pool of individuals who have missed opportunities to thrive in a world swayed by bias and prejudice. A vast majority miss out on the beauty and color and possibilities that diversity adds to our society. Does a healthy, thriving forest consist of only one type of plant, one species of animal or insect? Or is it made up of a boundless variety all working together to live and thrive? What a blindfold humans wear!

3. Build bridges and be astute

Remember, there are only two people in the world: you and others. The "others" are usually on the "other" side of you, and you must build bridges to connect with them. Those who see clearly are intentional about connecting with others. They do whatever they can to establish links between themselves and others. In fact, they work toward developing or belonging to a network of people. Clear-sighted people see opportunities in others. This astuteness drives them to develop relationships and build bridges to connect with people despite how different we may all seem.

When it comes to human connection, there are five categories of people. The first category is the skeptic. The skeptic is wary of connecting with anyone. Their initial reaction to new people is one of distrust and caution. People may become skeptics either because of their experience or background. Some people are products of relationship disappointments they have not been able to overcome, therefore making it difficult for them to trust anyone. Their past creates the blindfold that prevents them from seeing others clearly. In other cases, some may have grown up in a home or environment of suspicion and distrust. A lack of trust becomes engrained in their mindset, making it challenging for them to see others clearly. The skeptic does not generally build meaningful relationships.

The second category is the needy. The needy recognize the importance of relationships but do not reach out to build them. They sit and wait for others to connect with them without taking any personal responsibility. The needy accuse you of not calling them or reaching out to them. They sometimes feel neglected by others and place the obligation of building relationships and bridges on others, not themselves. The needy do not build meaningful relationships due to their one-sided approach: their "all-about-them" approach. Those who are needy do not see others clearly.

The third category is the sporadic. This category of people includes those who build relationships and bridges just because of what is in it for them. They do not make permanent friends with anyone. They reach out to you when they need you and pull away when they decide you're no longer needed. You may think of them as opportunists. They do not care about a relationship if there is no immediate benefit in it for them. The sporadic will be with you in the days of plenty but will opt out when things get tough. In many cases, the sporadic cannot see beyond their own nose.

The fourth category is the grouchy. The grouchy cannot maintain a relationship. They are touchy, hypersensitive, and sometimes irritable in their approach to others. This category tends to burn bridges, sometimes even the same bridges they themselves built. They would rather lose a friend than lose an argument. The grouchy do not care about how another person feels about a relationship and sometimes think that others are too sentimental about it. The grouchy will end up having no one around them, no one to live life with, because they have pushed everyone away. Those in this category lack the ability to see others clearly.

Those who see others as being valuable and important to their own journey build and keep healthy relationships.

The fifth category is the wright. A wright is a builder. Those in this category have an intuitive understanding of the value of relationships, and they do everything they can to build them. It is good judgment to know that we cannot achieve any great thing singlehandedly and that we will continue to require the contributions of others to succeed. Those who see others as being valuable and important to their own journey build and keep healthy relationships. The wright do not just build relationships, they become the link between other people.

You have probably heard that you have only about two or three degrees of separation from the person or persons you need to succeed in life. And the truth is, we may all be only some degree of separation away from one another throughout the world. Have you imagined how successful you could become if you had direct access to almost anyone you needed to contribute to your journey to success? If you are a businessperson, this may mean you have access to all the skills, all the capital, all the advertising, all the salespeople, and all the customers you need. Could you imagine how successful the world would be if we all had clear vision and could use our insight to connect with anyone in the world to help them succeed and in turn help yourself succeed?

Although human potential is extensive, most people will realize only a small fraction of what they are capable of in a lifetime. Therefore, everyone has areas of strengths and areas of weaknesses. Others are talented and skilled in areas where you are not. We need other people to complement us in our areas of weakness. We need to not only see others clearly, but we also need to see ourselves clearly. Seeing yourself clearly requires that you identify what you lack, be willing to acknowledge the lack, look for people who will complement you in your lack, and be willing and humble to work with people. That is why we form teams and families and cities and work in synergy.

There is no one person that has it all, but our society is arranged such that each one of us possesses something needed by someone else. In that case, we should be clear-sighted enough to locate the missing pieces, which may require that we also release what is in our hands to others. Seeing others clearly and gaining insight into how other people impact our lives should help us overcome skepticism, neediness, lack of commitment, and hypersensitivity such that we become relationship builders.

4. Engage with others and be the solution

The purpose of seeing people clearly is to be able to act based on their perspective, not yours. This is crucial. As I mentioned earlier, a lack of clear-sightedness is the reason we see a serious abuse of authority and power around the world, leading to dysfunctional leadership at every level. It is the reason many people lack success and why society does not function optimally. Those who cannot see with their insight do not solve problems, they only create more problems.

You and I have a responsibility. Without clear-sighted leaders, the cycle of mediocrity will continue. We cannot force others to take off their blindfolds, not even our leaders, because one must be ready to do so on their own. Therefore, one cannot be ready to make real progress in their life until they can see others clearly. Take that a step further, and even leaders cannot be ready to make real progress in society and the world until they can see others clearly using their insight.

Those who cannot see with their insight do not solve problems, they only create more problems.

So, let *us* break the cycle of parochialism that keeps people in mediocrity and embrace insight and sound judgment instead.

Sometimes, being the solution may mean nothing more than finding a hand to hold. Using that as an example, think about your journey from the earliest time you can remember until now. Could you have made it this far without any help from anyone? I know some people had much less help and went through many difficulties; I get it. However, any breakthrough we achieved still involved the participation and benevolence of others in some way. Those people likely saw us clearly, the same way we need to see others clearly so we can hold their hands.

That leads me to this thought: does being clear-sighted about others then *require* us to find a hand to hold? Perhaps becoming clear-sighted means helping someone achieve what they may not be able to achieve on their own. We may need to do something freely for someone for which they are unable to pay us back. The help we give others becomes a source of hope and inspiration. When we help someone achieve something important, we are telling them they can do it successfully and building them up for greater things. And when we do that, are we not also achieving inner success? Does our sight not get clearer with each person we help, with each hand we hold?

Meanwhile, supporting others does not mean giving them handouts without any sense of responsibility. It rather means that you rally round someone who is trying and is committed to their cause with resolve and determination to succeed. After all, everyone is responsible for the outcomes of their lives.

However, it takes someone with insight, perception, and judgment to notice the needs of others, find a hand to hold, and inspire hope in others. Be the solution.

See Yourself Clearly

This is something that can be easily overlooked. Many people are unable to see others clearly because they cannot see themselves clearly. You are unlikely to be able to give what you do not have. You have probably heard that you should love your neighbor as you do yourself or do unto others what you would like them to do unto you. Your disposition to other people, how you see and treat them, is directly related to how you see yourself. The way you see other people reflects how you see yourself, deep inside. How do you see yourself?

How you see yourself becomes obvious to people around you through your expressions and actions.

More importantly, the clarity that you have in seeing yourself determines how effective and successful you will be in your business, career, and personal life. Do you think everyone knows who they really are? Not at all. Many people know their friends, family, or pets better than they know themselves. Your outward expression is usually a reflection of how you see yourself, the insight you have about yourself. How you see yourself becomes obvious to people around you through your expressions and actions.

As I discussed elaborately in my book, *Pursuit of Personal Leadership*, you cannot assume a self-identity that you have not mentally adopted first. How you express yourself starts with the way you see yourself and how you think about yourself. Until you begin to see yourself clearly, your ability to succeed will remain limited. You cannot function optimally without seeing yourself clearly. Most people are not even aware of what they are capable of; their own potential is obscured by their lack of insight.

How you see yourself with respect to who you really are could be represented by the top figure shown at the end of this section. Your hidden true self, represented by the circle on the right, is endowed with gifts, talents, and abilities that cannot be appraised. Inside of every one of us resides a bank of hidden potential. Note that it is impossible to draw a boundary around your true self as human potential cannot be capped. Meanwhile, most human beings will neither discover nor tap into a significant portion of their potential in an entire lifetime. Many people will die without realizing, developing, and exploiting their gifts, talents, and abilities because they are unable to see themselves clearly.

Your mentally adopted self, represented by the circle on the left, is on a journey to self-discovery. It is possible for someone to adopt a self-identity that does not reflect their true self. Most people's thoughts about themselves these days are disjointed from their hidden true self. They adopt, in their minds, an identity different from who they really are. That is why you see people who think very little of themselves and try to be like someone else or place a limit on their own ability to become successful in their endeavor.

The middle of the figure is the intersection between the two circles, which represents your true self that you have intuitively discovered and allowed to dominate your thoughts about yourself. Your goal, and my goal, should be to continuously shift the circle on the left toward the right as in the second figure at the bottom. We must become clear-sighted about our own hidden potential so we can mentally become who we truly are. When we open our inner eyes, our insight, to who we really are, we give ourselves the opportunity to thrive in the world.

Here is the key. Every single one of us has an incredible amount of hidden potential abilities. The potential abilities become visible only when we discover them. We discover and find ourselves only purposely through insight and intuitive understanding. Only a few people will discover their potential abilities by accident. When we see ourselves clearly, then we can tap into, develop, and exploit who we are so we can positively transform various aspects of the human experience. We change the world through what we do with our gifts, talents, and abilities.

When we open our inner eyes, our insight, to who we really are, we give ourselves the opportunity to thrive in the world.

In fact, an important definition of leadership is the ability to discover oneself, see our potential, develop and deploy our gifts and talents, take self-responsibility for the outcomes of life, and inspire others to discover themselves too. Anyone that does that is clear-sighted. They become influential and we call them a "leader."

Seeing yourself clearly through insight and intuitive understanding enables you to see others and the world clearly. It broadens your vision of yourself and the world around you. It helps you take off the blindfold, enabling your inner eyes to see what your physical eye cannot see.

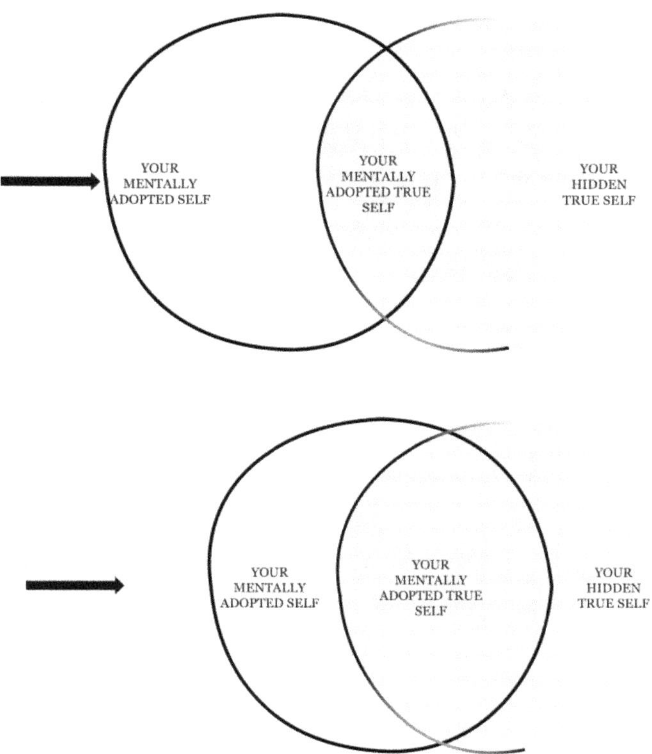

Figure 1: *How you see yourself with respect to who you really are*

CHAPTER 1 SUMMARY

The tale of the incident in the Dwumati Forest of the Awalaffe Kingdom illustrated how two people view their situations differently based on their needs, experiences, preferences, and understanding. Then you were asked if you took sides in the incident. Did you? We all see things from our own perspectives most of the time. And we usually see other people on the other side of the equation.

Meanwhile, we must unlearn the self-centeredness we all inherited from birth and alter our perspective about other people. The light we throw on others determines how we see them. Therefore, to see others clearly and cure our blindness, we must be willing to do the following:

1. Learn the real meaning of respect.
2. Remove biases and obliterate prejudices.
3. Build bridges and become connectors.
4. Engage with others and be the solution.

Each person must also see themselves clearly, constantly discovering and tapping into our own true self.

Chapter 1 Action Items

Think about what you have learned in this chapter. Think about your frame of reference. Think about your perspectives, how you see others and how you see yourself. To help you determine what to do going forward, go through the following action items and complete each section as required.

1. Write the names of five individuals that work closely with you at your place of work or school. In front of each name, write five good (or potentially good) things about the person. Focus only on the positive and do not make any assumptions. Comment about your experience trying to determine what is good about others. Then decide to always see only the good in others.

---

2. Take a moment to examine yourself closely with insight and sound judgment and see if you have made any decisions based on bias or prejudice. Most of us have done so, whether consciously or unconsciously. What would you do differently moving forward? Then write down three things we can all do to obliterate prejudice.

---

3. Building healthy relationships is important for a healthy state of mind and for our success. Remember that you have only a few degrees of separation from those you need on your journey. Write the names of five individuals or groups you will intentionally build bridges with. How would you go about developing those relationships? What is the purpose of relating with those people or groups?

---

4. Think about the circumstances and the people around you. In what three ways can you be the solution to the needs around you? Consider your team, coworkers, or family.

5. What remarkable thing have you discovered about yourself recently? Is there anything great or wonderful you

know you can do but you have only contemplated repeatedly? What about your gifts and talents? Write down a few. How can you continuously develop your strengths?

CHAPTER 2

Finding Your Rich Expanse of Gold

Laduro sat still as a rock in his wooden lawn chair on the first-floor balcony of his old inherited house, holding a goblet of local palm wine supplied by his friend, Delani. Poor Laduro gazed over the lump of cedar he had cut the previous day while the wine seeped down his throat into his empty stomach. He kept wondering what it would take to sell the new bundles of wood he was preparing. The year was almost over, and the dry season was imminent, a season when families and food sellers stocked up on wood before it began to rain again the following year.

I wonder why everyone prefers to buy wood from Alaje, the rich merchant of Irefin, and not from me, he thought before falling further into his musings. *I have tried to succeed in this wood business too, but nothing is working for me. I still owe Delani for the amount I borrowed from him to buy equipment last year. I left masonry to try this new business with the hopes that the gods would favor me this time. It seems to me the gods have predetermined who will find fortune and who will perish in penury. I am surely not on the list of those whom the gods have blessed. I can neither provide adequately for my family nor afford anything of value. Unless the gods review my case and reappoint fortune in my favor, I am doomed to fail and suffer,* Laduro lamented.

He shifted his gaze from the pile of wood to the sidewalk to the right of his balcony. There, leaning against the corner pillar, was Delani. He had been there for some time, unnoticed by his friend, who was wallowing in despondency.

"Why do you sit there moping like someone without hope for the future?" asked Delani.

Laduro did not respond. He just sat mute, lost in his own thoughts.

Delani continued. "I have also thought deeply about my situation. I am not satisfied with the meager money I make from wine tapping. I have struggled all my life. However, I am sure there is light at the end of the tunnel. I think we just need to learn what successful people do and do it. Perhaps you and I could go on a search to discover what the rich and the successful do. Let us look for answers. It may even be that the gods would bestow upon us a rich expanse of gold."

At the possibility of finding a rich expanse of gold, Laduro leaped out of his chair. "Could we not consult Fadayo the Oracle, who bears words from the gods? Perhaps he may tell us what fortunes await us in our search for answers?" he asked.

Delani agreed it was right to consult with the oracle before embarking on their journey to look for answers. Perhaps the gods would bestow blessings and favor upon them.

The following day, the duo left Irefin for Oke Adu to consult with Fadayo, who told them the gods had already spoken to him before the friends' arrival.

"The gods have indeed favored you both," Fadayo said. "The gods have allotted a rich expanse of gold to each of you. The tides are turning in your favor. But it is your responsibility to seek and find what you have been allotted. You must each find the pathway to your riches. Your destiny lies in your own hands," the oracle added.

The friends thanked Fadayo with a gift of two young ducks and left immediately.

"I have always known I am destined to discover a rich expanse of gold, but how could the gods not tell me exactly what to do and where to go? If the gods truly wanted to help, should they not just show the way? Should they not just send the emissary of goodness to deliver fortune to the one they favor? There is no prospect in my work, yet I have no one to help raise me up. The tides are surely turning, but in others' favor, not in mine," Laduro bemoaned to his friend as they crossed a small brook on the way to the center of Irefin.

In reply, Delani posed a question: "Does divine destiny not require one to open their mind to see the opportunities around them? A person who seeks to gain insight into the way of success, who searches for the pathway to riches, will eventually find it, so I understand Fadayo's words. Such a one possesses an enviable future. As for me, I can see the tides turning in my favor. I can see the sunshine."

They parted company, each to his own house at the junction of Irefin and Oje.

The two friends continued their lives, each one holding tightly to their perceptions. Eventually, seven years passed. Both Delani and Laduro remained good friends through the years, but they had made opposing decisions.

After those seven years, a group of four young people from Irefin's chess club, a community of chess players Laduro was a member of, came to visit him. Not long after their arrival, Laduro began telling his appalling story. Near the end, he paused for a moment to try and turn so he could lie on his side rather than his sore back. He had been at the healing house in Irefin for about four weeks, having contracted a rare disease that was eating him alive.

He seemed to have given up on himself, as he spoke like someone in the departure lounge of life. "I did not regard or adhere to the oracle's instruction," Laduro told the group. "I believed in my own foolishness, thinking riches are divinely allocated without any personal responsibility. 'Isn't the pathway to riches bestowed by the gods that of unmerited favor?' I'd thought to myself. I believed that whomever the gods smiled on should wait, and wait some more, until fortune came knocking at their door. So I waited and waited, doing little, marking time, until poverty became my best friend. I became overwhelmed by the debts I owed to friends and neighbors. I buried my head in shame as I endured the mockery of those who surrounded me. I lost hope, fell into depression, and became terribly sick," he complained.

"How about your friend, Delani, who you mentioned went with you to the oracle? What happened to him?" a young lady asked.

"Ha, Delani is a wise man. He told me what he would do with the oracle's declaration and warned me, but I disagreed with him," retorted Laduro.

Delani had taken the words of the oracle seriously. He had sought every opportunity to learn more about his chosen wine business. After working hard at it, he now possessed the most profound knowledge of where to find the best wine in the land. He studied where his customers were and what they wanted. He sought opportunities to work with others to serve his community the most expressive wine.

Six months after the visit to the oracle, one of Delani's customers, Alaje, the rich merchant of Irefin, recommended him to his associates in Oja-Oba, who sold wine to the land of the queen of England. Delani became a successful wine merchant who employed hundreds of wine tappers, owned fifteen wine-processing plants, and exported wine to twenty-five countries.

So it was that Delani prospered through his astuteness and hard work. He showed his belief in the declaration of the gods by taking responsibility for finding the opportunities around him and working hard to secure his allotted fortune, a rich expanse of gold indeed.

Sitting on a Gold Mine

Just like Delani, do we not possess the ability to make a fortune using what we have and through what we do? You may not need to own fifteen wine-processing plants, found Tesla or Amazon, become the CEO of Apple, or inherit the royal wealth of Abu Dhabi. However, each of us possesses something with which we can make a profit. The challenge for most of us is that our lack of insight, the inability to see clearly in our minds, makes us miss great opportunities. Every human being can possess a rich expanse of gold by using their insight, perception, and judgment. This ability is within everyone.

Opportunities exist in all trades, professions, career paths, and businesses. These opportunities can be realized through insight, the clear-sightedness of the mind, but the lack of insight will always result in the belief that the grass is greener on the other side and the continued search for the next best thing.

Every human being can possess a rich expanse of gold by using their insight, perception, and judgment. This ability is within everyone.

Here is a secret most people don't know: the bright future or success you are looking for is not ahead of you such that you need to chase after it, but it is trapped inside of you such that you only need to discover it and work at it. This principle is true irrespective of your life's work. Locked within each one of us is an enormous amount of potential with which we can bring about great results. We just need to look inward, using our insight after removing our blindfolds, to unearth our own ability and then apply ourselves to our endeavor.

When you look at yourself in your current vocation, work, profession, or business, how do you see? Do you see opportunities or a lack of opportunities? When you look at your current location or situation, how do you see? Do you see bounty or lack? Here is the truth: how you see determines what you get. Those who see with their eyesight see problems, obstacles, and impossibilities; those who see with their insight see opportunities and possibilities. What a disparity!

Some of the most sere, desolate regions of the world have been transformed into paradise because certain people saw a paradise in a naturally dry land, Dubai for example. Conversely, although not always the case, we have seen lush, fertile, and arable regions of the world reduced to war-torn, poverty-stricken zones because of a lack of insight, perception, and judgment.

Is it not the same with individuals? No one can naturally succeed without insight and judgment. This is because we direct our efforts toward what we personally see and know, not toward what we are oblivious of. What you do not know cannot serve you. In fact, what you do not know, what you are ignorant of, can affect you adversely. Ignorance is not a virtue. People expend futile effort when they lack the right perspective and insight, when they act without clear-sightedness. We must continually strive to know more.

Russel H. Conwell presented an excellent example in his 1915 classic work, *Acres of Diamonds*.[1] It is a story of an old farmer who lived in Pennsylvania in the 1800s, around the time when the first oil well in North America was arguably discovered in Canada. In his search for something better than his farming business, this farmer became attracted to the oil business and decided to sell his farm and seek employment with his cousin, who was in the business of collecting coal oil, a fossil fuel used as an illuminant in the nineteenth century.

Adopting a wise approach, he did not sell his farm until he was able to convince his cousin, who was reluctant to hire the farmer due to his lack of knowledge in the oil business. The farmer, again wisely, had to study the subject until he became knowledgeable enough for his cousin to agree to hire him. He then sold his farm for a decent amount: $833, which today would be around $30,000.[2] And off he unwisely went, with no thought for what his farm, his current surroundings and circumstances, could offer. He thought the grass would be greener elsewhere.

Not long after he left, the new owner was out preparing to water the cattle when he noticed the previous owner had done something unusual. Behind the barn was a brook, across which the previous owner had put a plank of wood on its edge a few inches into the surface of the water. The plank appeared to have been there for several years, with the apparent purpose of redirecting a layer of a dirty-looking substance to the opposite bank as the cattle would prefer to drink from the clean, clear water downstream.

Here is the bombshell ending. The original farmer who had gone to Canada had been using that plank to dam a torrent of coal oil to one side of the brook so the cattle could drink from below, and had been for twenty years. Geologists from the

State of Pennsylvania later declared the discovery to be worth several billions of dollars. In fact, the first successful oil well in the United States was drilled on August 27, 1859, by George R. Bissell, Jonathan G. Eveleth, and Edwin L. Drake right on that farm.[3,4] Yes, in Titusville, Pennsylvania. Drake, a colonel and driller, was the one who struck oil there for Seneca Oil Company, which was founded by Bissell and Eveleth.

The initial owner of the territory on which Titusville stands, the farmer, was said to have studied everything about oil: the look, smell, taste, and how to refine it. Yet he had not seen it on his own farm. He had looked outward, not inward, so he sold out, for only $833. What a misfortune!

Before judging the misfortune of the farmer, take a minute to think about yourself. Perhaps that story is like yours or you are about to make the same mistake. Are you currently sitting on a gold mine without knowing it? Look around you. I mean look with insight, rather than eyesight. Look using your intuition, using the clear-sightedness of your mind. What do you perceive? How do you see? Many people have missed opportunities of a lifetime because, again, the pasture always appears greener on the other side. Before shifting direction, making a move, changing jobs, leaving a marriage, switching a business, choosing a direction, or starting a journey, ask yourself if you are seeing your current situation clearly. Are you looking inward or outward? Are you using your insight or your eyesight?

Does that mean we must all stay where we currently are because what we are looking for must necessarily be where we are now? No, not at all. The main point is that we need to see beyond what is obvious. Those who discover and do great things are those who look with their third eye—the intuitive and perceptive eye of the mind—uncovered. Successful people see what others don't see because they see with their insight.

Do we not all sit on a gold mine? Here on Earth are enormous amounts of resources, assets, and riches. They are everywhere, but only a fraction of people see them. Some of the treasures of the earth are tangible, while others are intangible. There are opportunities all around us irrespective of where we are and what our circumstances are. We get ahead in life by identifying and exploiting those opportunities for ourselves and others. A rich expanse of gold is not given as a handout. It is discovered by those who can see clearly. Do you see clearly?

Those who discover and do great things are those who look with their third eye—the intuitive and perceptive eye of the mind—uncovered.

Invisible Mental Twinning

In the story of the Titusville farm, there was a physical farm with hidden physical treasure. However, there are instances when we need to see beyond what currently physically exists. Successful people often see the invisible and then bring the invisible into reality.

You have probably heard that imagination is everything. Humans are only limited by their imagination. You might have also heard that if the human mind can conceive it, then humans can achieve it. That is why many incredible things have been achieved in the world. Every wonderful thing we see today once existed only in someone's imagination. They resided in the imagination of those who saw clearly, whose minds believed the unbelievable and saw the impossible.

All inventions, creations, innovations, achievements, goods, services, and systems are a mirror image of what once existed in someone's mind. I call this concept "invisible mental twinning." Just as in technology, where we have what is called a digital twin, a virtual digital representation of an actual physical process or system, so too do we all have a mental twin: a mental image, or an imagining, of a reality we can come to experience in the world.

The mental twin of anything is as real as the actual thing. A mental twin is not inferior to the physical thing just because it is intangible. For example, if you create a mental picture of obtaining a college degree in your mind, and you nurture that imagination for long enough with the determination to achieve it, you can actualize that mental picture. In that case, what you conceived in your imagination is as real as obtaining the actual college degree until it becomes tangible.

Successful people arrive at their destination in the invisible world of mental twinning before starting the journey in the physical realm. They continually harness the power of mental twinning guided by insight, perception, and judgment—clear-sightedness—to create a better future for themselves and others. How could you create a clear picture of future possibilities in your mind? Then how could you actualize the dreams even when the circumstances surrounding you suggest the contrary?

Do you want to be successful as a leader, businessperson, worker, team player, or contributor wherever you are, even within your own family? Then learn the concept of creating an invisible mental twin. Mental twinning of future realities is something we can all learn. It all starts with deploying our imagination and being guided by intuition and insight.

Seeing Opportunities Clearly

I was speaking with a friend a while ago when we fell into discussing the story of a man who had built one of the biggest business empires of the twentieth century by exploring a viable alternative to his original intention because he saw what someone else did not see. This is his story.

Conrad, the son of a Norwegian immigrant to America, was born in 1887, raised in New Mexico, and became a hardworking, enterprising, imaginative, and outgoing young man.[5] He started working full-time in his father's merchandizing business at the age of sixteen, delivering goods and supplies to ranchers throughout their territory. The core skills he learned in the business included bargaining, trading, and managing credit risks. Conrad also learned to endure adversity and tough times, having worked with his parents to endure a serious financial set-back in the period before World War I.

Young Conrad spent his early life searching for a calling. He tried politics, public speaking, and banking before joining the army when World War I arrived. After his commissioning as a second lieutenant, he served in San Francisco, Washington State, Boston, New York City, and Paris. He was discharged from the army in 1919 after receiving the news of his father's death. Nevertheless, he kept searching for his calling until, at the age of thirty-one, he started feeling a sense of failure.

Conrad's mother, like many mothers, continued to support her son, encouraging him to find his own frontier. This was the time of the Texas oil boom. Conrad wanted to explore the opportunities, so he traveled to Cisco, Texas. His mission was to invest in a bank in Cisco with whatever he had left. However, the deal he was pursuing fell apart. He needed a place to stay for the night. Therefore, he turned to the run-down Mobley Hotel in Cisco for accommodation.

Meanwhile, Conrad had a remarkable experience at Mobley Hotel. Many oil workers sought accommodation at the hotel, such that long queues grew daily. Staff had to sleep in eight-hour shifts as the hotel was so full of oil workers. Many people needed to look for accommodation elsewhere because the hotel was always full. The hotel owner was tired of the work and wanted to retire, having no plan to expand. The owner just wanted out of the business. Well, it was one of those times when you are in the right place at the right time. Conrad heard that the hotel owner wanted to sell; that was his wake-up call. He gathered $40,000 from family and friends and the Cisco Banking Company to buy the supposed flophouse. That was the beginning of what is now widely known as the Hilton Hotels & Resorts.

Conrad Hilton bought his first hotel, the Mobley Hotel, in Cisco, Texas, in 1919. He went on to improve the hotel drastically, adding more rooms and employing more effective services to manage the business. The first hotel to carry the Hilton name, the Dallas Hilton, was bought by Conrad Hilton in 1925. The business continued to expand from there on. As of 2018/19, Hilton Hotels had a portfolio of eighteen world-class brands, comprising over 6,800 properties and over one million rooms spread around the world.[6]

Don't miss the main point of the Hilton story. Conrad Hilton was in Cisco to invest in the banking business. His plan failed, the door had closed, but his mind was open. He saw an alternative opportunity, which eventually became his frontier. The same hotel that the owner had seen as burdensome and difficult to manage Hilton saw as the foundation for building a great business empire. It was obvious that the hotel owner saw things with his eyesight, focusing on the problems and the difficulties, while Hilton saw the same situation with his insight, paying close attention to the opportunities.

What do you do when your plan fails or when you do not get what you want? Do you sit there complaining and explaining away your failure? If Hilton had decided to continue complaining to his friends and family, explaining how miserable he was when his plan fell apart, he would not have been able to see the Mobley Hotel opportunity clearly. Life's failures sometimes becloud our sight and prevent us from seeing clearly. When things do not work the way we planned, then it is time to create an alternative plan. Those who see clearly with their intuition, perception, and judgment are not surprised by failures. They accept that failure had been a possibility, then open their inner eyes to the opportunities that lie ahead.

Apart from the alternative opportunities discovered during a time of difficulty, sometimes great opportunities come to us in times of success and comfort, disguised as less attractive possibilities. It takes clear-sightedness, a completely open mind, and forward thinking to identify those opportunities.

In my book, *Pursuit of Personal Leadership*, I discussed how success can stand in the way of success. One reason many people are stalled and unable to move forward is that they allowed today's success to get in the way of tomorrow's achievements. They see themselves as having "arrived." Therefore, they stop thinking intuitively and miss greater opportunities for success. Let me give you a practical example from the modern business world.

Around the year 2000, Blockbuster was a company basking in the glory of its own success. This was back in the days when its DVD-by-mail business was thriving, and the company was making a fortune. In those days, you could walk into physical stores to rent DVDs or request delivery to your address. Headquartered at the Renaissance Tower in Dallas, Texas, Blockbuster made $6 billion with its 9,000 rental stores worldwide. Conversely, there was Netflix, a two-year old start-up company distressed after the dot-com bubble and struggling to make a profit from its online DVD rental business.

Netflix cofounders Marc Randolph and Reed Hastings, together with the company's CFO Barry McCarthy, had sought the attention of Blockbuster's management team for months, to meet and discuss a possible business deal. Eventually, Blockbuster's CEO John Antioco and his team invited the Netflix executives to a meeting in Dallas. According to Hastings, the Netflix situation before the meeting was such that their losses that year would total $57 million, and they were eager to make a deal; they had worked for months to get Antioco to respond to their calls.[7]

At the highly anticipated meeting, the Netflix executives made their pitch. They asked Blockbuster to buy Netflix, then allow them to develop and run the online video-rental arm of the merged business: Blockbuster.com. Although Hastings and his team believed there was a great future for online business as technology would improve significantly, Antioco thought otherwise. He believed the dot-com hysteria was completely overblown. In fact, Ed Stead, Blockbuster's general counsel, explained how every online business, including Netflix, was not sustainable and would never make money.[8]

After much debate, the inevitable question came. How much did Randolph and Hastings want Blockbuster to pay for Netflix? The answer was $50 million. The Blockbuster executives declined the offer without making a considerable counteroffer. The rest of the meeting went south from there. There was no bargain, no deal.

Thereafter, Netflix stayed the course, and two years later, in 2002, went public. The company had pivoted from online DVD-rental services to internet streaming services. By 2019, Netflix had over 167 million subscribers in 190 countries and started producing their own TV shows and movies. As for Blockbuster, who was then a hundred times larger than Netflix, the older company declared bankruptcy in 2010 after the world had moved away from the DVD-by-mail model. By 2019, except for the one remaining Blockbuster video store in Bend, Oregon, the company had become history, having been unable to adapt to the online streaming model.

Becoming clear-sighted enables us to see into the future through insight and perception, such that even in times of success and abundance, we can continually ensure our own future.

That was another profound lesson, right? The Blockbuster-Netflix story is another reminder that we need to see beyond what the outer eyes can see. Seeing with insight requires a complete 360-degree view of the current situation in the context of possible future realities. Becoming clear-sighted enables us to see into the future through insight and perception, such that even in times of success and abundance, we can continually ensure our own future.

A Seven-Step Recipe for Finding Your Rich Expanse of Gold

Now we know that when people discover their frontiers using their insight, they prosper significantly. They strike a rich expanse of gold. Meanwhile, those who use only their eyesight have no idea exactly what to do in life; they must learn to employ their insight: their intuition, perception, and judgment, the clear-sightedness of the mind. Here I offer you a seven-step recipe for finding your own rich expanse of gold. This recipe is a personally experienced cure for a lack of clear-sightedness, a cure for your inner blindness.

1. Make mental twinning, the invisible mental construction of future realities, your habit. Always give deep and detailed thought to whatever you are doing. Do not start anything of significance unless you have carefully thought it through. Clear-sighted people are thoughtful, arriving at the destination in their minds before embarking on the actual journey.
2. Be willing to consider alternatives. Do not be rigid in the way you think. There is no one perfect way to succeed in life. Let your mind explore alternative ideas. Many people have found their frontiers and calling by being open-minded.
3. Have faith in your ability to succeed. Believe that you can succeed. Let the thought of success dominate your mental faculties. Always stay on the positive side of

your thought process even when you are aware of negative facts and limitations. Dwelling on the negative is a recipe for constant failure and eventual defeat.

4. Resist the complacency of those who wish for good things without backing their wishes with action. Only a fraction of people will ever find their rich expanse of gold. Why? Because most only wish for it without the determination to find it. Your great intentions and your imaginations must be accompanied by actions. Great things are not accomplished by divine handout but by the determination, dedication, and actions of those who have faith and believe the impossible.
5. Arm yourself with knowledge in your work, vocation, profession, or endeavor. You cannot afford to be ignorant. Knowledge illuminates the mind and fosters clear-sightedness. Knowledge becomes a lever for intuitive understanding and creates the basis for proper judgment in decision-making. One of the greatest ingredients for clear-sightedness is the pursuit of knowledge.
6. Be willing to endure the hardships that come while finding your own rich expanse of gold. Sometimes you need to dig wells in several locations before finding oil. When you dig and you find nothing, dig some more, and dig in other locations. Failure is not defeat. Quitting is defeat. Nothing of significant value comes cheap. Those who pay the price get the prize. A clear-sighted individual knows that every challenge is a steppingstone to something greater.

7. Be alert all the time, letting the antennae of your mind and senses catch the frequency of opportunities when they broadcast. For most people, this is a matter of doing the right thing at the right time in the right place. There are no real accidents in life. Those who continually position themselves to seek opportunities, who are alert, eventually sight opportunities.

CHAPTER 2 SUMMARY

With the story of the two friends, Laduro and Delani, who made opposing decisions after consulting the oracle, we found that everyone must take self-responsibility for finding opportunities and work hard to grasp one's allotted fortunes.

The challenge for most of us is that our lack of insight, our inability to see clearly using our minds, makes us miss out on great opportunities. This was the case for the old farmer who sat on an oil deposit for twenty years without knowing it and sold his property for a meager amount, though it was later found to be worth billions of dollars.

We must adopt invisible mental twinning and see opportunities clearly, just like Conrad Hilton and the Netflix cofounders did. We must allow neither failure nor success to becloud our view of opportunities. We must all learn and use the seven-step recipe for finding one's rich expanse of gold:

1. Make mental twinning your habit.
2. Be willing to consider alternatives.
3. Have faith in your ability to succeed.
4. Resist the complacency of those who wish without acting.
5. Arm yourself with knowledge.
6. Be willing to endure hardship.
7. Be alert.

Chapter 2 Action Items

Evaluate your life's journey based on what you've learned in this chapter. Think about your experience, what worked and what did not work. Think about the opportunities you've harnessed or missed. Then complete the following action items.

1. List three opportunities around you now. This may be a need you can help fulfill, a business or career opportunity, a relationship opportunity, or something else. Do not say there is none. You must look with insight and perception, with clear-sightedness, to find them.

   ----

2. For each opportunity above, write down three steps you can take toward them. Remember, doing nothing is more expensive than doing something. What is your first, second, and third step to take advantage of the opportunity you identified?

3. Re-read the seven-step recipe for finding one's rich expanse of gold. Which steps will be most challenging? Think of how you can improve in that area. Write down your thoughts. Finally, determine to master the seven steps.

CHAPTER 3

Darting into the Wild Is Key

It was a fateful summer, a season of scorching sunshine in the countryside of Leventia in the boreal forests of the northern occidental lands where Larry and his young family lived. Larry's adventurous family decided to spend the season exploring the forest trails of the Bay Mountains, a few hours from Leventia by road. It would be an exhilarating experience for the family.

School was over for Deman and his sister, Duelly. They were excited to load the trunk of the family's 1980 Oldsmobile Cutlass Cruiser station wagon with the items they needed for their summer trip.

"Should we take the new bow and arrow with us?" Duelly asked her mom, Lolla, who was just stepping out of the garage onto the driveway and carrying a box of food items.

"I'm taking my bicycle and bear spray," Deman interjected.

"You both know camping in the Bay Mountains requires adequate preparation, and you must take whatever you need. So, if you think you need it, bring it," Lolla responded.

Finally, everyone was ready to go. Duelly ran to the front door. "Don't lock the door yet, Mom! I left my novel on the couch," she said.

Larry, already sitting in the driver's seat, honked the horn a few times while asking everyone to get into the car. Duelly ran back outside with her book in her hands, and Lolla locked the house door. Everyone hopped in the car, and *vroom*! Off they went.

It took about two and a half hours to arrive at Camp Kellinghan in the Bay Mountains. It was around 5:00 p.m. on a Sunday evening. The family pitched their tent on Lot 75, close to the lake. The five days of camping and exploring promised to be excellent.

Deman and Duelly could not wait, so they threw on their swimsuits right away and spent two hours splashing around in the lake's shallows.

The family enjoyed hiking, scavenger hunting, mountain climbing, and camping during their holiday. Lolla particularly enjoyed spending time around the camp, contemplating nature and listening to the trees pulsating and insects buzzing. Oh, what a feeling!

The last day of their trip, however, was the most adventurous for the family. Larry and Deman went for a walk after lunch. They were about two miles away from their camp when Deman noticed a seemingly distressed creature lying under a large rock in the woods. He called for his dad, who was only a few meters away, to come take a look at the animal.

"What is it?" Larry asked Deman.

"It looks like a cub, a bear cub," Deman replied.

"Why are you still standing there staring if it's a bear cub? We may be in danger if the mother is around," Larry asked.

"No, the cub seems to be alone and distressed. I looked," said Deman.

Larry peeked beneath the rock at the animal, who looked very weak, as if it was suffering from dehydration.

"What should we do, Dad?" Deman asked.

"I have a great idea," Larry replied.

After a minute of deliberation, the unbelievable dad and son made what one may term the most dangerous decision: they picked up the bear cub. Larry wrapped him in his coat, and they ran back to camp. Does that sound like a dumb idea? Well, that may be true, but that is what they did.

When Larry and Deman arrived at the camp, they ran up to Lolla, who was sitting on a wooden stool; Duelly stood beside her. The two had packed all the family's items in the car and had been waiting for the two men to return so they could head back home.

"What made you run as if you were being chased by a ghost?" Lolla asked as she glanced at whatever Larry had wrapped in his coat.

Larry unwrapped the bear cub while he looked for a small cup and water. Deman told the story as Larry managed to use the cup to pass water down the small creature's throat.

"We must leave this place immediately," Larry declared.

Isn't it strange that they took the cub with them?

Nevertheless, they got in the car, and Larry drove off. The initially dehydrated bear cub looked revived after drinking some water. He sat on the floor of the car, looking like an abandoned puppy.

"You know we must call the conservation officer. You shouldn't have picked up the animal in the first place," Lolla told Larry.

"We're not calling anyone. Deman and I have a plan," Larry responded.

The family arrived home that evening. It became a quiet evening as Lolla wondered what her husband and son were up to, and Duelly was dumbfounded by the whole idea of bringing a bear cub home.

Two days later though, it seemed the whole family had come to terms with their new adventure, raising the bear cub like they had raised their dogs, feeding him domestic food and treating him like a member of their household. They even named him Dart.

Months went by. Dart kept growing like all baby animals do. He ate with the dogs, played in the garden, and behaved just like any tamed animal. He grew quickly through the winter.

In Leventia in the spring, it was customary for wild cats, wolves, and bears to edge close to farmyards and residences in search of food after months of winter hibernation. Larry's family would let out their animals after the snow had melted and give the dogs a chance to roam the large front yard. But something odd happened that year.

Dart encountered a group of bears in the treed portion of the front yard, just about a mile away from the house. He had seen himself in the living room mirror several times in the past and realized that the bears looked exactly like him. He was surprised the first time he saw one and ran back into the house. No one noticed Dart's first encounter with the wild bears.

The same thing happened a few times in the same week when the wild bears neared the house again. Dart loved his human family but knew he looked more like the bears. So, he contemplated joining them to explore the woods for a while. He did so and enjoyed their company but returned home not long later.

Three weeks later, unnoticed by Larry or anyone else, Dart went into the woods with the bears. This time, he made an important decision: to explore who he saw himself as. He had come to see himself as a wild bear, so he darted into the wild where he believed he belonged. Off he ran, never to return home again. He was, after all, a bear.

Three nights went by. Dart was nowhere to be found.

On the third night, the whole family gathered around the backyard firepit. They waited for Deman to start the fire as they prepared to roast marshmallows. After about fifteen minutes, the fire began to die down, retaining the glowing coals, the ideal fire for marshmallow roasting.

Everyone sat quietly around the fire for what seemed an hour. They were as quiet as a praying congregation. Lolla decided to break the silence. "You seem bothered by Dart's disappearance," she said to Larry.

"Not exactly," Larry responded. "I've just been pondering the lessons I've learned for the past few hours, and I think I finally have things figured out."

Intrigued, the whole family sat closer to listen to what Larry had to say as they continued roasting and eating marshmallows.

Larry had put his musings to poetry and called it *Larry's Factum by the Marshmallow Fire,* an ode that teaches us to dart into the wild. He recited it then for his family:

Like Dart, so many of us
Live under circumstances that shaped our ideologies
Until we see ourselves as we truly are,
Until we decide to explore who we are.

Their life's calling, some may find
In the environment that shaped and molded them,
Living to embrace the ideals of their early lives,
Growing on the same path they were raised on.

But dart into the wild many will have to do,
To live the identity they desire and dream of.
Who they truly are they shall discover;
Who they're meant to be they shall become.

An intrinsic self we all possess,
The true self that cannot be forever tamed.
When ourselves we begin to clearly see and become,
We can impact and change the world.

It matters not what system shaped you,
Your environment, religion, or the world at large,
You have a duty to know and express
Your intrinsic self that cannot be forever tamed.

The tears in Lolla's eyes became contagious. Duelly and Deman joined the sober reflection. Larry reclined in his lawn chair and relaxed as the coals in the firepit turned to ashes.

"I will write this experience as a story and call it *Dart into the Wild*," Deman said. And he did exactly that, sharing the story until it went viral.

The Systems that Shaped Us

Everyone has a personal philosophy. What is your personal philosophy? Your philosophy becomes the window through which you see the world. Every decision you make reflects what you believe. Unless you are under coercion, you act based on your beliefs. Those beliefs are formed over a long period and are, in most cases, difficult to alter.

> ***Every decision you make reflects what you believe.***

Let us ask a profound question. What is the origin of one's beliefs? We need to think deeply about this question. How did anyone arrive at their philosophy? Why do you see the world the way you do? What shaped your beliefs? It turns out there are many factors responsible for shaping the beliefs of an individual. These factors form the basis of the personal philosophies of people that have changed the world for better or for worse. Let us look at a few origins.

1. Your home environment

I stumbled on a South African version of the TV show, *Family Feud*, with the renowned American comedian Steve Harvey a while ago. Steve asked the contestants why one would light a candle. To his surprise, the number one reason to light a candle in South Africa was electricity load shedding. He needed to ask his audience what that really meant. Well, it meant that the power distribution company would switch off electricity for a few hours in different neighborhoods to balance the load; there wasn't enough power for everyone at once.

I thought Steve would understand the rationale for load shedding, but he said this instead: "That's stupid. Who thought of that? There is a lot of electricity." He was right. Steve was born and raised in the United States of America, where load shedding does not exist. What appeared normal to the people of South Africa appeared stupid to him.

Let us leave South Africa and travel to other developing parts of the world. Have you ever wondered why people who live in many developing countries continue to tolerate abject poverty and governmental resource mismanagement? To answer that question, you may need to consider Maslow's hierarchy of needs. At the very bottom of the hierarchy is the need for survival: food, clothing, and shelter.

Someone who hasn't been able to feed their family is probably not concerned with the launch of a rocket to somewhere in space. The philosophy of such an individual is reduced to that of survival. They will vote for any politician that guarantees them the bottom of Maslow's hierarchy of needs. Those who understand this, who know the truth, and are willing to break the cycle of poverty in those countries are usually in the minority. The politicians understand this, and they keep the majority in penury so they can keep manipulating the people in every election. The cycle of poverty continues. The people become victims of their environment. Guess what happens when one of the oppressed, whose psyche has been demoralized, gets a taste of power? They oppress others in turn and the cycle continues.

Whether you acknowledge it or not, your philosophy is shaped by environmental factors. The society in which you live, your family, your upbringing, your social circle, the schools you attend, the books you read, and the media to which you are exposed all shape your philosophy. There is the tendency for everyone to become a product of their environment. If you expose yourself to a certain environment for a long time, you will begin to think and behave like that environment. This is powerful stuff.

Here is what I want you to do. Examine the environmental factors surrounding you and determine if your thoughts, beliefs, and philosophies are shaped by them or not. Meanwhile, no one is meant to live as a victim of their environment. That is where clear-sightedness comes into play. To be clear-sighted is to seek the knowledge that helps you see the world the way it really is, beyond your environment and your view through your own window, and to see your true intrinsic self.

To be clear-sighted is to know enough to break free from negative background influences and to exploit your gifts, talents, and abilities. To be clear-sighted is to realize who you are so you can dart into the wild and change the world.

Humans have one fatal flaw, and it's at the heart of all historical issues and is still one of the biggest problems plaguing our world today. People are conformists. They are like a liquid that takes the shape of the container that holds them. Most people allow society to mold them without being conscious of it. And parents allow their children to be shaped by society, by the philosophies of both their families and the strangers around them. This is the reason people live an average life. Average thinking leads to average living. Unless one becomes clear-sighted, they cannot rise above the average level of success in their society.

We are here to shape our environment, to guide our culture, to influence others, and to command positive change in the world for the good of society.

Those who prosper see differently. They see the world clearly and see themselves differently from the average mediocre personality invented by their environment. After all, whether you know it or not yet, we are not here just to be shaped by our environment, we are here to shape our environment, to guide our culture, to influence others, and to command positive change in the world for the good of society.

2. Religion and its tendencies

It is not news that religion has shaped our view of the world and ourselves both positively and negatively since the beginning of recorded history. Many people are products of their religious beliefs and faith. Religion usually roots deeply in people's belief systems, such that it trumps most ideas outside that belief. That is why people will go to extreme lengths for the sake of their religious convictions. Religion is a window through which an immensely substantial number of people see the world.

It is generally believed that people are victims of religion as an accident of birth. That is largely true. Someone born into Christianity is likely to be a Christian. Likewise, someone born into Hinduism is likely to practice the religion. Why? Because what shapes us at the earliest part of our lives has lasting effects on our beliefs and consequent philosophies. It is difficult to separate people from their background influences. That said, we also know that many people have converted from one belief to another by embracing new ideologies.

What does this have to do with insight and clear-sightedness? One of the downsides of religious practices is the dogmatic nature and the impact of that on one's ability to see clearly. Religion can become either the blindfold preventing one from becoming successful or a source of life and liberty for another. Successful people see clearly enough to contextualize their religious beliefs for their own spiritual well-being and the good of society. However, those who are blind follow religious ideologies without thought or question and promote unfounded beliefs, thereby missing opportunities and maintaining a myopic view of the world around them.

People should more often question religious beliefs that violate the conscience, liberty, safety, and well-being of others. And the purpose of religion should be redefined as a platform for one, and for society, to perform good deeds for others. Those who do this and make society better will attract success and prosperity to themselves. We must do away with the hatred, division, inequality, and destruction perpetrated in the guise of religion. Those who perpetrate evil under the pretense of religious practices lack insight, perception, and judgment; they lack clear-sightedness.

The question for you and me is, "How do we see past religious lines?" We might have been influenced by the religious beliefs that shaped us, which is not wrong. Religion offers many benefits too: community, morals, guidance. However, everyone is responsible for their behavior and the outcomes of our lives, which requires seeing religion from the perspective of sound judgment, insight, and perception, not fanaticism and blindness. Everyone is free to question their own beliefs, think critically, and arrive at a personal conviction that guarantees the good of society.

Meanwhile, religion is no longer the most-used opium of society as it might have been in the past, though it is still near the top of the list. The whole world is now overdosing on another narcotic called social media.

3. Social media and the virtual world

In the recent past, say in 2010, most wouldn't have thought social media would become what it has become today. It is the new environment in which we live. A 2022 report in *World Economic Forum* suggested that an average internet user in the world spends two hours and twenty-seven minutes per day on social media, with numbers differing widely by country.[1] Countries in the emerging market with a significant percentage of young people, for example Nigeria and Philippines, topped the list with the average social media user signing in for slightly more than four hours per day.

What do users do on social media? Or rather, what do you do on social media? Most people basically spend their time consuming content like you consume food. Surely, information is to the mind what food is to the body. However, the intriguing part of the social-media brouhaha is how consumers take the content in like some form of addiction. Mobile devices continue to show notifications and sound pings all day, with the owners unable to go without checking them every moment. It is like someone addicted to drugs who can't do without it.

Everyone is at liberty to feed on whatever they like on the internet, especially on social media. Social media contains loads of information and misinformation, more than we can even imagine, all of which only serves to further divide us. As a result, whether consciously or unconsciously, social media is shaping people's lives and destinies. Given the amount of time each person spends on social media, you can be sure that people's philosophies and the consequent outcomes of their lives are now being controlled by it.

In my award-winning book, *Be a Change Agent: Leadership in a Time of Exponential Change*, while discussing the future of learning, I explained how it is everyone's responsibility to be selective about what they learn on the internet. We are now living in a virtual world, where everyone can create and share content of any sort without evidence or support. It takes insight, perception, discernment, and judgment—clear-sightedness—to censor the large amount of information bombarding an average individual every day.

You do not need all the content on social media. Every advertisement is not for you. Every video, audio, reel, message, post, chat, emoji, ping, story, or photo is not for you. Every doorbell is not sounding at your door. You need to put your activities in the virtual digital world into perspective. Yes, your philosophy will be shaped by it, but you need to consciously participate in the process by placing a filter below the content you allow to drip into your mind and shape your philosophy and your life.

The point is that the way you see and use content on the internet and social media will determine the philosophy that will guide your life, just as with religion and upbringing. You see the world through the lens of the social-media content to which you are exposed and through the perspective—the lens—of those who have posted that content on social media. Social-media content can then form the basis of your beliefs and actions. Therefore, you must navigate this virtual world with clear sight, with insight, perception, and judgment.

Nothing Changes until You Change

Going back to the story of Dart at the beginning of this chapter, we could conclude that we can change our situations by seeing ourselves clearly and then taking action. Dart saw himself—his ability, potential, nature, and strength—clearly and decided to dart into the wild to become the new person he had found within. How do you see yourself? Do you need to dart into the wild?

An average person wants to improve their personal situation. Everyone is looking for a better home, a better friendship, a better job, a better car, a better life, et cetera. Humans seem to be naturally wired to wish for a change or an improvement in their situations.

But nothing improves by chance. The only law of life that guarantees improvement is the law of change. Nothing improves without change. The challenge most of us face is that we are okay with everything else changing except us, whereas nothing changes until we change, and that includes a change in the belief systems that have shaped our philosophies.

> *The only law of life that guarantees improvement is the law of change. Nothing improves without change.*

For example, without change happening in our attitudes and perspectives, we are unable to significantly change anything about our situations. Those who consistently experience improvement and success understand the law of change. They know that nothing changes until we change it. Yes, there are inevitable changes that are not within our control. However, we have the capacity to determine our response to life's ever-changing situations. At the same time, an internal change of mindset and attitude will help us change our external situations and responses to the issues life throws at us.

This change of perspective created by a change in attitude and mindset is possible only when we see ourselves, the world, and our situations clearly. We must rip off our blindfolds, cure our blindness, change course, and take on our true self, the intrinsic self that cannot be tamed and can only be seen with insight.

See the World Clearly

The world is made up of the systems that govern it. We can think of the systems of the world in terms of governments, public systems, organizations, associations, infrastructure, legal frameworks, religions, industries, societies, and families. Every one of us relates somehow with the systems of the world in which we live. If we are alive, we are inseparable from the systems.

Successful and impactful people, and truly great minds, see clearly enough to know how to navigate the world's systems. They have sufficient insight and judgment that enables them to live at peace with the systems around them. They understand when to fight, negotiate, or withdraw. They do not see the world as their destination but as an ephemeral port of call, a place to make impacts and better the lives of others as their limited time of life passes away.

Have you ever wondered why Nelson Mandela became the classic example of authentic leadership in the history of our world? He was not the only one who struggled for freedom. He was not the only one imprisoned for fighting for freedom. South Africa was not among the first countries whose leaders fought for independence. So what makes the Mandela story unique?

Mandela was clear-sighted enough to understand the purpose of forgiveness and reconciliation in post-apartheid South Africa, and he did all he could to pursue peace and unity. In his 1990 Christmas message, Mandela said, "We must all strive to be inspired by a deep-seated love for our country, without regard to race, color, gender, or station in life. We must strive to be moved by a generosity of spirit that will enable us to outgrow the hatred and conflicts of the past. We must anchor all our efforts in the common determination to build a South African society that will be the envy of the world."[2]

Despite spending nearly twenty-seven years in prison, along with other freedom fighters, Mandela discouraged retaliation, enmity, or any form of retribution. His beliefs and actions were in consonance with his clear-sighted view that reconciliation does not mean forgetting or trying to bury the pain of conflict but working together to correct the legacy of past injustice.[3] What an informed, mature, and insightful way to see the world!

While Mandela was only one example of how to see the world clearly, given the multifaceted dimensions of the world's systems, you and I need to continuously open our minds to the realities of the world we live in. The world's systems do not serve well those who work against the principles that govern the world. None of us can be a law unto ourselves without repercussion. When we learn the principles that govern the systems around us, and we align our actions accordingly, then we position ourselves to prosper and make positive impacts in the lives of others.

Some may argue that there is much injustice in the world, that the world's systems do not guarantee freedom, equity, and peace for everyone. Yes, that is largely true, and it is the reason the world needs you. What is your life's endeavor? What is your vocation, profession, career, or interest? What can you do to improve humanity in that area? When you look at the systems of this world, how do you see? How would you employ your insight and perception to identify what we lack in the world and be the solution?

The world needs clear-sighted leaders now, more than ever before. You and I need to become the source of illumination for the world, breaking down the parochial and myopic view of the systems that govern the world and focusing our insight to see the world clearly and align ourselves with its systems with an open mind and heart. We must flow smoothly in and out of the systems with noble intent. It is time to become an agent of positive change in the world.

We have, for the most part, become products of the systems that shaped us. However, it is our duty to seek and strive to know who we really are, such that we can become our true self. We are at a crossroads, an intersection of systems and reason, a point where we decide if we want to hold on to every ideology that shaped us or employ our reasoning to see the world through insight.

To accomplish this, some people will need to free themselves from limiting beliefs and narrow-minded philosophies, while others will just need to dart into the wild to become their true self. Yet for others, it will be a matter of continuous reinforcement and growth in the trajectory they have found themselves on. Whatever your situation is, you must see the systems of the world with your inner eyes as you journey through this life. You must see the world clearly through your intuition, insight, perception, and judgment, thus ripping off your mental blindfold, curing your blindness, and seeing with the eyes of your mind.

CHAPTER 3 SUMMARY

Larry's family had a remarkable encounter in the wild, in the forest of the Bay Mountains. But they could not tame Dart, their newfound family member. As his name implies, Dart needed to dart into the wild and become who he was meant to be. Similarly, your own intrinsic self cannot be tamed despite the philosophies that might have shaped you. Although your personal philosophies might have been shaped by your environment, religion, social media, and the like, it is still your responsibility to see clearly enough to break free and dart into the wild.

Nothing changes until you change, and it all starts with seeing the world clearly through insight, perception, and judgement: clear-sightedness. Some people need to free themselves from the limiting beliefs and narrow-minded philosophies they have learned. Others need to dart into the wild to become their true self. Yet others need continuous reinforcement and growth in the trajectory they have found themselves on.

Most importantly, you and I need to become the source of illumination for the world, breaking down the parochial and myopic view of the systems that shaped us and the systems that govern the world and focusing our insight to see the world more clearly with an open mind and heart. Flow smoothly in and out of the systems with noble intent. It is time to become an agent of positive change in the world.

Chapter 3 Action Items

Look in the mirror like Dart did, then work on the following action items.

1. How do you see your intrinsic self? Write a statement that describes the way you see yourself. Is the way you see yourself enhancing or limiting your ability to thrive? Think deeply about this. Your goal should be to realize who you really are, to exploit your own potential. It all starts with how you see yourself.

----

2. Write down three or four factors that have influenced your thinking or philosophy and how you see the world. Everyone is influenced by one thing or another. Think about your background, associations, environment, religion, social media platforms, etc. Write

down and analyze those influences and how they shaped the personality you project.

3. Using your analysis in question 2 above, identify the influences you would like to correct or alter. Think about how you can unlearn and relearn to reshape your philosophy. Do you need to change your environment, religious associations, or the information to which you expose yourself? Write down two to three actions you will take.

4. Ultimately, make a resolution to grow, break free, or dart into the wild. Write down a three- or four-step plan for darting into the wild.

CHAPTER 4

Hitting Rock Bottom Is a Good Thing

Jerry hurriedly pulled his Volkswagen Beetle into the first open stall in the car lot in downtown Turnville, an ordinary little town. The place was already jam-packed with vehicles. It was happy hour on Friday night. Jerry's friends had been waiting at the rotunda close to the fountains at Plackade Resort to celebrate his new job as sales manager at Confere Paints. They would drink into the night as they celebrated Jerry's promotion.

You may think this is a happy ending. Sadly, it's not. It's but the high point of a life typical of those without clear thinking. It is the peak before the fall to rock bottom.

Four years earlier, when Jerry had finished high school, he could not continue his education like many of his mates had. He still had many options though. Rather than studying at a university where the cost of education was too much, he could have gone to a trade school and started on a path to becoming a journeyperson. However, attending a trade school did not appeal to him. He wanted to study engineering, architecture, or business like his high-school friends, but neither he nor his parents could afford college or university.

So Jerry decided to look for a job, any job. He first started as a storekeeper in a small bicycle shop near their home in Turnville. He arrived at work on time, took his work seriously, learned quickly, and helped many of his colleagues pull through the day. Within weeks, his industriousness came to the attention of the store's owner, Claire. He then got an opportunity to work in sales and to manage cash. He worked in the bicycle shop for two and a half years. During that time, Jerry provided some financial support to his parents and saved a significant part of his earnings, hoping to return to school sometime in the future.

Meanwhile, Claire saw much potential in Jerry and realized the small amount of money he made at the bicycle shop would not keep him there much longer. She decided to recommend him to Confere Paints to assist in their sales department. Willy, Claire's husband, owned Confere Paints, which was the largest paint distribution company in the Turnville area. What a great opportunity for Jerry!

As expected, Jerry did quite well at Confere Paints. He supported his colleagues in the sales and marketing departments. He learned quickly and was trusted with many of the company's major clients. By then, Jerry had earned enough money to live on his own. He rented a studio apartment in downtown Turnville, close to his work. He kept supporting his parents and had even saved almost enough to return to school.

Jerry applied to study business administration at the University of Turnville and was accepted, but something happened that changed his plans. The same weekend Jerry received his admission letter from the university, Willy invited him for golf and a walk in Turnville Park. During the walk, Willy asked him if he would be willing to head the sales department and become the company's sales manager. Jerry told Willy he would think about it and give him a response in the following week.

This situation posed a dilemma. Jerry knew his salary as a sales manager would beat that of any graduate in engineering or business administration. He had been working for four years and had gained some experience. Many of his high-school mates would graduate before he returned to school to start where they had begun four years earlier. He thought, *If I return to school and graduate from university, I will be looking for this same type of job in another four years, the job I already have.*"

So he decided to take the job at Confere Paints.

Jerry returned to work the following week and told Willy of his decision to take the job. By the end of the week, he had received his appointment letter and a fat sign-on bonus. He used his sign-on bonus to buy a new Volkswagen Beetle and started his new life. He declined his university admission. As expected, his parents were somewhat disappointed by his decision not to return to school, not even on a part-time basis. But their concerns did not bother him at all. He had jettisoned his plans for school.

A few months later, Confere Paints started struggling financially after losing a legal battle with a customer. The situation brought the company to its knees. The struggle continued for a year, after which the company became insolvent and filed for bankruptcy. You're likely already thinking of what became of Jerry—and yes, you are right—he lost his job.

The situation was devastating for Jerry, but he decided he would move on. He could not afford to waste time as he had used all his life savings as a 50 percent down payment on his new house. He had also married his high-school girlfriend, and they had started a family. He started applying for sales-manager jobs but did not meet the basic requirements in most cases, that being a diploma or degree in business or a similar field. He became frustrated.

After three months, Jerry connected with his trusted friend, Currie, who sold typewriters. Currie persuaded him to invest in the business and become a partner. Using the equity on his house as security, Jerry turned to his bank to borrow money for the business. As he was an excellent salesperson, he did quite well in the first few months. The partners expanded their warehouse and bought hundreds of units and continued selling.

The way Jerry saw it, he would be the sales genius and Currie would be the marketing guru. However, Jerry was wrong. This all happened at a time when computer technology was taking off. Many companies and individuals had moved away from using typewriters to using computers. The demand for typewriters began to fall, and within one year of Jerry's investment in the business, they had lost 80 percent of the company's value. The two business partners had not pivoted into the computer business on time, so they struggled because of serious competition. They soon went out of business.

Eventually, Jerry lost his investment. He also lost his house to the bank as he was unable to pay either his loan or his monthly mortgage payments. Due to his constant disregard for his wife's advice, she left him and took their daughter with her. Jerry was back to ground zero. He sold his car, moved out of the house, and rented a small room in an old house in the inner city. He lost everything he had worked for. He could not believe what had happened to him.

After some weeks of worrying about his predicament, Jerry realized he could start all over again. He decided to revisit his earlier plan to return to school if he could. The plan was different this time. He would work in the evenings and on weekends and study during the day. He was admitted to a diploma course in commerce at the School of Skilled Trades of Turnville. He also started working as a sales assistant at a local clothing store. It was difficult to juggle school and work, but he gave it a try.

As the pressure of schooling became intense, Jerry could not concentrate much on his survival job. He got fired. He worked in a few other places but couldn't keep up with work and the pressure of school. He dropped out of school in the middle of the second term as he was unable to gather enough money for tuition. He was again back to ground zero.

On the day he dropped out of school, he got a dreadful phone call: his parents had been involved in a ghastly motor accident. His dad died at the scene of the accident, while his mom was rushed to the hospital, unconscious. After a week, his mom also died.

On the night of his mom's death, Jerry thought, *I am now at rock bottom. I do not know what to do. This life is unfair. I have lost everything, and I am unable to start again. I used to be the envy of my friends and colleagues, but I am now a laughingstock. I am doomed forever. This life is not worth living.*

That night, he returned to his room in the rickety old house, confused and downcast. He saw himself as completely beaten, battered, and finished. He could not see himself rising again and was blind to new possibilities. He pulled out his shotgun, the only thing of value he had left.

Is it not better to die than to wallow in misfortune and bury one's head in shame? he thought as he sat on his battered old couch, weighing his situation.

What do you think? Should he just end it there or try again?

When You Are at Rock Bottom

What does it mean to be at rock bottom? Rock bottom is the state of one's least possible happiness in life. It is the lowest possible point and the worst-case scenario. Everyone's rock bottom is unique to them. What one person considers their rock bottom may not be the lowest level for another, depending on their experience, disposition, and personal attitude to life.

When you get to a point where the going gets toughest for you, making you feel like you are at the end of the road, you could be at rock bottom. Rock bottom is the verge of completely giving up. It is the point where most people abandon their journey, throw away their confidence, roll back their dreams, or give up on life.

Rock bottom causes people to become demoralized because of its effect on the psyche. Sometimes, rock bottom makes one doubt their own ability, skill, expertise, or worth. The journey to rock bottom makes people feel hopeless. Once someone has given up, it becomes challenging to help them see clearly. Those at rock bottom may not see clearly enough to deal with their situation. In fact, at rock bottom, most people forget the good times and the blessings they have enjoyed in the past and only focus on the problem at hand. Someone at rock bottom may see things only from the perspective of their bad experiences and not be able to see past their failures.

Meanwhile, the salvation for one who has given up and is at rock bottom is a change of perspective. The solution is to build up new hope with clear-sightedness. If someone at rock bottom can see their situation clearly with insight, perception, and judgment, they can eventually rise above the challenges. They will see the opportunities in the world around them, even the opportunities existing within their failure. The key is to see with insight rather than eyesight. Those who look through their eyesight will see only how big their problems are, whereas those who look through their insight will see new possibilities. Possibilities are always bigger than problems.

I remember my teenage years in southwest Nigeria during the political turmoil of 1993 and 1994 following the annulment of the June 12, 1993, general election by military dictators. The situation was devastating to many. The aftermath of the annulment was a serious economic, social, and political crisis. Everything was shut down in most major cities. The supply chains of most commodities ground to a halt. There were riots everywhere and many people were killed. It was a case of a country being at war with itself.

Those who look through their eyesight will see only how big their problems are, whereas those who look through their insight will see new possibilities.

My middle-class civil-servant parents lost their salaries for several months. They had six mouths to feed but things became difficult, and it was similarly difficult for many other families. We all switched to survival mode. We lived on whatever we could find. There were days when you would wait for vegetables and corn to grow right before your eyes so you could eat. I remember the hardships of those days and the dark nights of wondering whether the situation would end one day.

I saw what my parents were going through at that time, their disappointment and sense of failure. However, I also saw their resilience and their sense of purpose and hope. I saw the strength of people who believed the impossible. They taught us to believe the impossible and hold on to our faith. And we lived. As you would imagine, the situation did not last forever.

Life is made of high points and low points. You can imagine your journey through life like someone traveling through a landscape of mountains, valleys, forests, rivers, obstacles, expressways, rough patches, rocks, sand, fields, level ground, et cetera. You will likely experience many, if not all, the features of that landscape. How you really experience your journey and your arrival at rock bottom is determined by your perspective: *how* you see, rather than *what* you see. What each of us experiences in life is important but not as important as the four perspectives we all share. If you remember these common perspectives and work to see them clearly beyond your problems or failures, you will be able to see more clearly with your insight.

Let us discuss the perspectives that we share, especially at the lowest points in our journey. Whenever you ask, "How should I see when I am at rock bottom?" remember each of these four perspectives:

1. You are not alone

When you hit rock bottom, know that you are not the first to go there and you won't be the last. It is a perspective we all share at one time or another. Life is full of ups and downs; it's a journey where success is fabricated from the raw materials of failure, challenges, and problems that must be overcome. There is really nothing new here in this world. If you are going through a tough time and you are at the lowest point, rest assured there are other people in the world going through the same or a similar situation. More importantly, there are people who have left that experience behind them and have emerged on the other side. Perhaps Jerry needed someone to remind him that he was not alone.

While there is no promise that things will always turn out the way we wish, having the perspective that challenges are normal and that problems are interwoven with success in life will help one see their situation clearly. The difference between someone who gives up at rock bottom and someone whose hope is alive is their perspective. One person may not accept that things could get so bad and feel sorry for themselves, while another may understand that challenges can come in an overwhelming fashion but can still be dealt with.

> *The difference between someone who gives up at rock bottom and someone whose hope is alive is their perspective.*

Here is the point. You are not the only one at rock bottom. You are not the only person to have ever been there. You are one of millions of people at their lowest points and one of billions who have experienced it at some point. How each person emerges on the other side of the challenge depends on their perspective, on how they see. It is not so much about what is happening and why life has selected us for the situation, it is more about how we see with our minds. It is about insight, perception, and judgment.

2. You have only one direction to go

If you are truly at rock bottom, the lowest point in your life, then the only other direction you can go is up. Think about it this way. Assuming you were at the top of a hill and you started falling, you may keep falling until you reach halfway.

There, you have the option of either climbing or falling further. If you keep falling, you may eventually reach the valley. In the valley, there is no other way to go. The only other direction you can go is uphill. If you don't want to remain in the valley, you must determine to climb the hill.

Resting in the valley is the same thing as being at rock bottom. Nothing is lower; the only direction you can go is up, by climbing. There is a better chance of increasing success for someone in the valley than for someone atop the mountain. Those on the mountaintop can fall, but those in the valley, at the bottom, cannot fall further. That tells me rock bottom can be seen as a place of opportunity for climbing up, a perspective shared by only those who are clear-sighted.

Those who see clearly see opportunities for upward movement, while those who lack insight continue to wallow in their despondency. It is all about how each person sees and perceives their situation.

3. It does not last forever

When you are at rock bottom, know that this season does not last forever. No matter how serious the challenge may be, nothing lasts forever here in this world. It is all about perspective. It does not matter whether you have moved from failure to failure or from challenge to challenge. Sometimes it even feels like the best opportunities in life have eluded you, and you think you have missed the best moments of your life. Yes, you might have missed great things. However, the best things in life are always those yet to come. Change is part of life.

As I mentioned earlier, the salvation for someone at rock bottom is a change of perspective. Those who give up at rock bottom have concluded their journey is over, whereas the game of life is not over until you give up. When you look, how do you see? Do you see the game as over or do you see the game beginning? It is a perspective. It is like waves on the ocean. Forever they ebb and flow, high and low, though they never stop. It is the same with your life. Changes come. Failures and successes wash in and out. Ride the waves of life and change your perspective. See with your insight.

You cannot afford to hold on to your past and let the past drag you into hopelessness. Press the reset button. Dream again. Start again. In fact, start all over again.

You cannot afford to hold on to your past and let the past drag you into hopelessness. Press the reset button. Dream again. Start again. In fact, start all over again. Approach your situation with insight, with the clear-sightedness of your mind.

4. It is a solid foundation

Have you ever considered why it is called "rock" bottom? Yes, it is a rock. If you keep falling until you reach a rock, then you can be assured that you cannot fall further downward. But that is not all that there is to it. Rock bottom becomes a solid foundation upon which we can build. Before reaching rock bottom, you would have gone through certain experiences. You would have possibly learned patience, perseverance, and resilience. You might have survived negative emotional conditions. You might have learned to live with little or nothing.

In most cases, the journey to rock bottom allows us to build character through what we experience. It is like going through the school of life. What we learn on the way to rock bottom becomes part of our foundation. Even if your mistakes, foolishness, or negligence are what got you to rock bottom, you can learn from them and become a better individual. When you are at rock bottom, that means you can now start building on a solid foundation. At the very bottom is the bedrock, the solid platform on which to build. That is the perspective of those who conquer their situations.

When we go through positive experiences, things feel normal. We enjoy the pleasure of seeing things work our way. However, when times are hard and we face disappointment, nothing feels normal. We may ask if our efforts and attempts at success are worth it.

Let us face the fact that it is not usually easy to overcome disappointment. If you have ever put your best foot forward and tried to do something big but faced a brick wall in the end, you probably understand what I am saying. Depending on our responses, those disappointing experiences can either help us grow or discourage us.

As I mentioned earlier, one thing is certain: rock bottom is not permanent. We become stronger through what we experience. Like I once heard Steve Harvey say, "Behind every moment of adversity, there's a lesson and a blessing." In whatever circumstance we find ourselves, we must not miss the lesson and the blessing. Failure is not final. It is a rock-solid foundation upon which to grow new opportunities.

What we experience during a disappointing time, at rock bottom, presents us with an opportunity to iterate our actions as we implement the lessons learned. Sometimes things do not turn out the way we expected. However, we will be able to make sense of a situation that does not make sense if we adopt a big-picture approach.

Are you going through a tough time now? Just keep moving forward as you learn through the experience. Focus on the blessings as you learn the lessons. See the opportunities that lie ahead. Stand tall on the bedrock and you will build something that stands stronger than ever before.

One Thing You Must Not Allow

I came across an inspirational story I want to share.[1] It was the experience of Alex Wheatle, who, at the age of eighteen in 1981, was arrested, charged, and sentenced to prison alongside six others at Camberwell Green Magistrates Court in south London for assaulting a police officer. Alex's father had abandoned him at the age of two. He grew up in the notorious Shirley Oaks Children's Home in Croydon. During his sentencing, relatives of the other six accused sat in the court room in support of their own. But for Alex, no one was present. According to him, he suddenly became resentful because he had never felt so alone as in the moment he gazed across the public gallery at the court.

While being taken away in the prison van, Alex tried to think of a quick and easy way he could end what he described as his pathetic life. He eventually ended up in HMP Wormwood Scrubs in west London, where he described the jangling and clanging of keys and doors, respectively, as being much louder in the prison environment than elsewhere. Upon arrival, he was given his prison uniform, escorted to his cell, and pushed inside. As he heard the closing doors, he started preparing himself for the suicide he had mentally committed in the van.

Alex shared a prison cell with Simeon, who appeared to be about twenty years older. They had a hard time relating at first as Alex refused anything Simeon offered, instead preferring to wallow in his own self-pity as he devised a way to end his life. However, Simeon persisted in trying to become a friend, which led to serious tension between the two, then a physical fight that resulted in Alex being seriously beaten. Meanwhile, for Alex, the pain Simeon had inflicted was not as bad as the pain he felt inside, the pain of childhood abuse and trauma. The young man described himself as being very close to breakdown, in other words, rock bottom.

Alex was fortunate. Simeon was still interested in his story and insisted on hearing it during one of their many long nights together. Finally, Alex agreed to tell his story. Simeon seemed to understand Alex's disconnection from his roots, culture, and family, given the abandonment as a little child. The older man decided to reconnect the younger to his roots using the vast wealth of experience and learning Simeon had gained over the course of his life.

Simeon generously shared with Alex stories, novels, songs, and materials that helped him understand civilizations in Africa, the struggle for black liberation in South Africa, the fight for the equality of Black people in the Caribbean, and the birth of the civil-rights movement in the US. Although Alex's education had stalled after many suspensions and three expulsions from school, he could read quite well. He had been reading comics and magazines others discarded on the floor in his dormitory from the age of five.

Alex would later admit he hungrily consumed any novel or text Simeon gave him: Charles Dickens, James Baldwin, Richard Wright, Langston Hughes, John Steinbeck, and more. His reading helped him discover that he was not the only one having a tough time figuring out how to start in life. Alex didn't feel alone anymore; he started seeing himself with insight and perception, with clear sight. He eventually got his life back.

Just before Alex completed his prison sentence, Simeon gave him this instruction: "Alex, your life, and all those of the underclass, is just as valuable as anyone else's in this world; never forget that."

With Simeon's instruction stuck in his memories, Alex went on to become a writer. He started writing reggae lyrics and poems related to his experience and eventually became an author of several books, with a grateful heart for the opportunity to have met Simeon on his journey.

Have you ever been seriously beaten down? Does it feel like you are being beaten down right now? Life sometimes deals us a heavy blow. There is no guarantee that we will not face challenges. No one can promise you that you will never fail. In fact, life is interwoven with successes and failures, with good and bad times. The reason many people stay down when they have been beaten down is because of how they see their situation. Life has its challenges and disappointments, but you cannot afford to quit because you failed. You must get up and try again and then try some more. You cannot allow the challenges of life to completely inundate you.

Remember that when you are in the valley and you refuse to stay there, the only other direction to go is uphill. Every valley experience can be overcome with an uphill experience; the choice is ours to make.

> ***Life has its challenges and disappointments, but you cannot afford to quit because you failed. You must get up and try again and then try some more.***

I have decided to keep trying, and trying some more in different ways, until I succeed. For me, there is no giving up. What about you? Will you allow your problems to define you or allow the bashing to keep you down? Yes, there are real challenges in life, but they are there to be overcome. We can all choose to rise above the storms and soar like an eagle.

You must not allow yourself to become demoralized or totally hopeless when you are at rock bottom. There is surely light at the end of the tunnel, and when your time comes, it will seem like a dream. Yes, your time is here. Get up, look with the eyes of your mind, and take your place. Your new perspective will build new opportunities on that solid-rock foundation.

CHAPTER 4 SUMMARY

If you feel like you're going through a hard time, perhaps your story is like Jerry's. He started out well, with lots of hope for his future, but he ended up beaten, confused, and downcast. After many attempts to rise again, he reached rock bottom and gave up altogether. He is on the verge of making a crucial decision, and he needs you to help him out. Would you give up? Alternatively, how would you climb back up if you were him?

We sometimes find ourselves at rock bottom, in the worst situations of life. The experience we go through reaching rock bottom may becloud our judgement of our own situation, leaving us demoralized and unable to save ourselves. When you are at rock bottom, you must open your inner eyes to four shared perspectives:

1. See and know that you are not alone.
2. Believe and accept that there is only one direction you can go from rock bottom: up.
3. Remind yourself that no matter how difficult, the situation cannot last forever.
4. Believe that rock bottom becomes a solid foundation upon which you can build a tower of success.

You must not allow yourself to become demoralized or feel totally hopeless when you are at rock bottom. There is surely light at the end of the tunnel. Open your inner eyes and use your insight to see the possibilities.

Chapter 4 Action Items

Your story may not be exactly like Jerry's. Pause and evaluate your rock bottom, then reflect on the four ways of opening your inner eyes. Then work on the following action items.

1. Think about a particular rock-bottom experience you had. Write down four key lessons you learned through the experience. How have those lessons helped you to become stronger?

----

2. Are you currently at rock bottom? Remember you have only one direction to go when you're at rock bottom. Start choosing the bricks to build the foundation to get back to the top or shout out for help. Get up and rise above the situation. To help you do that, write down three steps you can take to start climbing. Also remember there may be challenges associated with going uphill, but you must determine to overcome them.

3. At rock bottom, you may need support. Who can you reach out to? Alternatively, try activities that can build you up, i.e., reading books on positive thinking, praying and meditating, joining the company of people with success mindsets, exercising and resting, maintaining an attitude of gratefulness in all circumstances, helping other people, or supporting worthy causes.

CHAPTER 5

Creating an Interruption in Forever

The Grand Master sat on His throne in the palace of Forever. An indescribable flood of light brighter than the sunlight shone overwhelmingly throughout the palace from His awesome presence. The light seemed to occupy the palace in an infinite space but at the same time in nothingness. The Grand Master was in the company of the innumerable nobles of Forever, governing with grace, peace, and justice.

Forever is a place of incongruent austere grandeur, with everything in perfect order and enveloped in the powerful light of the Grand Master. Everything in Forever exists by the will of the Grand Master, who is exceedingly fearsome and impressively awesome. He lives in the perpetuity of the lights of Forever because nowhere else could accommodate His awesomeness and predominance. The face of the Grand Master is perpetually out of sight because of the intensity of the light from His presence. His presence commands absolute respect, authority, dominion, and immensity. He is the Grand Master of everything.

Everything in Forever serves the desires of the Grand Master with magnanimity. No goodness surpasses the probity of the Grand Master, who is limitless in kindness, boundless in splendor, and eternal in authority. He deals in perfect justice with an abundance of love, veracity, and undeserving favor with the entirety of Forever. There is no imperfection in Forever because of the perpetual presence of the Grand Master, an absolute description of perfection and immortality.

Meanwhile, as perfect as it is in Forever, it is a particularly bizarre place. Although there is no word in our vocabulary to describe Forever, one may try to use the closest expressions that can be found. In Forever, everything exists in perpetuity and is eternal. Whatever is present in Forever has always been there and will continue to be there permanently. It is indestructible and constant, an everlasting existence of everything yet nothing. There is no matter, land, air, water, space, or anything material. The way to visualize Forever is through the never-ending lights shining from the presence of the Grand Master.

Everything in Forever remains immortal, permanent. Nothing can be undone. For example, were there ever to be an error—though that never happens—in Forever, it would be an everlasting error. If there was happiness in Forever, it would be eternal happiness. If regret were to find its way into Forever, it would be an eternal regret. Whatever anything is, it will remain there eternally. Everything is forever and ever.

That makes Forever an odd place. Everything in Forever exists in the moment of Forever, but the moment of Forever lasts forever. What a mystery!

By His authority, the Grand Master decided to cause an interruption in Forever and extend his sovereignty into the interruption. He decided to create a new order in which there would be a break from the eternity of Forever, where nothing would be bound to the perfection, perpetuity, indestructibility, and eternity of everything in nothing. Therefore, in an instant of eternity, the Grand Master released an unfathomable packet of His eternal light into a new order, causing an interruption in Forever. He interrupted eternity to create a beginning, which is the beginning of Time.

The Grand Master created Time to provide a break from Forever, to disrupt eternity. Everything existing in the new order operates in, and is governed by, the law of Time. Nothing can create or control Time in the new order. Everything must subject itself to the passing of Time. Time became a universal law of the new order.

The interruption of Forever and the consequent actuality of Time made everything in the new order possible; the formation of stars, galaxies, planets, oceans, rocks, and creatures all came into existence with the passage of Time. The material world of matter and energy came with Time.

More importantly, anything that exists in Time is not part of Forever and cannot exist in perpetuity. Anything subject to the law of Time is ephemeral. Our material world exists in Time, free from the eternity of Forever. What a relief!

Time as the Currency of Life: A Universal Law

You're probably wondering where this story is going. I also wonder. I've observed that an average person does not have the right perspective about the purpose, the main essence, of time. Most people cannot see the meaning and value of time. It is another kind of blindfold.

No, I am not here to discuss time-management principles and how to use schedules or priority lists. This chapter is not about how you need to rise early and work through your day with a checklist. My responsibility is to uncover the essence of time, why time exists in the first place. That understanding will help everyone become clear-sighted about their relationship with time, the value of time, and the need for time. The way you see time—with insight, perception, and judgment, or clear-sightedness—will determine how you will go through this world.

Let me start by stating that time and money are analogous to each other. Most of the qualities of money and time are the same, with only a few exceptions. For example, when you were born, you did not come with money. Well, unless you inherited a fortune. However, when you were born, you came with a certain but unknown amount of time. At any point in your life, you may know the amount of money you have left, but it is unlikely you will know the amount of time you have left.

The total of the unknown amount of time you live in this world is your own slice or portion of Forever, or eternity, within the existence of time. And that slice is extremely small compared to the entire amount of time that exists. Remember that I mentioned time is an interruption in Forever. Since the beginning of time, every event, thing, or creature has subsisted only within its slice of Forever, some for a few seconds, some for days, and some for billions of years. There have been billions of people before us, each one having completed their own minute slice of Forever, and there will be others after us, after we each complete our own minuscule portion of eternity within the existence of time.

Each one of us has an amount of time particular to us, whatever that is. One may argue that one can lengthen or shorten the amount of time they spend in the world. That is true. However, the main point is that just as we each possess different amounts of money, we each possess different amounts of total time in which we can exist. Two individuals may be born on the same day under the same circumstances in the same place from the same womb to do the same thing throughout their lives but with a big difference in the amount of time they may spend in the world.

Just like money, time is the currency of life. Time is how we spend life. With each second, minute, or hour we live, we let time pass.

Just like money, time is the currency of life. Time is how we spend life. With each second, minute, or hour we live, we let time pass. Yet time is different from money in the sense that you may decide when to spend money, but you cannot decide whether you will spend time or not. You may hold off paying your rent, but you cannot stop the passage of time. Time passes at a constant rate, the same rate for everyone. Everyone goes through the same amount of time in a day. We all go through the same amount of time in a year, even though we do not all have the same number of years to live.

Time is an atypical type of currency. The clock of life continues its clickety-clack irrespective of what you do or don't do. You cannot stop time. You cannot create time. You cannot control the passage of time. Meanwhile, there is one thing we can *all* do with time: we can guide and control our use of time. Like an administrator or a steward, we can oversee how our time is used. We may not control the passage or creation of time, but we can control our use of time.

Let us look at some ways we can oversee time as we do money, illustrating how we can control its use.

1. You can spend time

Just like money, time can be spent. The fact that we spend our time, whether judiciously or by squandering it, is a perspective that we all share. Someone who is clear-sighted enough to understand that time is the currency of life will control how they spend it. Every bit of time that passes is your slice of Forever that is gone, never to be retrieved. Would you not rather control how you spend it? Whatever one engages in serves to either move them closer to their dreams or further from success. There is an endless number of activities one can spend their time on, just like there is an endless number of things money can buy. What are you buying with your time?

2. You can waste time

If you were wondering where your time went, you don't need to wonder any longer. You probably wasted it. Anytime you cannot account for your time, or you use your time for something other than what you wanted or planned to do, something that does not bring any value to anyone or something that does not move you closer to where you ought to be, you wasted it. Just think about it. If you earned $1,000 this week and you only have $600 to put toward your plans or anything of value, you probably wasted $400. Do you account for your time? How much of it do you waste? The thought of having only a small slice of Forever should entice you to account for your time.

3. You can invest time

Whatever you spend your time on that helps you gain time in the future, make a profit, or enables you to be better positioned in life is an investment. For example, spending your time attending college is an investment in your professional life. Spending your time writing business proposals is an investment in your business future. Spending time educating and training your children is an investment in making them responsible citizens in the future. In fact, spending your time reading this book is an investment in removing barriers to clear-sightedness in your personal and professional life. Spending your time working hard in the earlier part of your career saving up for retirement so you can retire early is an investment in time to pursue other passions. How are you investing your time? In what are you investing your time?

4. You can save time

You save time by not spending all of it so you can have some left. Saving time gives you an opportunity to spend or invest the saved time later. The idea is that if you can take ten hours to achieve something, do not spend twenty hours doing it. Save the time and use it later. Some people are unable to get quality sleep because they cannot save time and use it for sleep. Saving time helps us do things we might not do when time becomes constrained. Do you save time? The opposite of saving time is wasting time, as discussed earlier. Saving time is a perspective seen with insight shared by those who see time clearly.

5. You can donate or give away time

Sometimes we spend time, not for ourselves but for other people or for worthy causes. Philanthropy shouldn't be only about donations of money. Those who donate their time for the welfare of others and use one of the most limited currencies—time—to volunteer and do great things should be given places of honor in society. It is too expensive to give time away. The reason is simple. You can earn more money, but you cannot earn more time for your day. The rich and the poor both have twenty-four hours in a day. Anyone that freely gives their time to help others, build society, train people, volunteer for charity, and support worthy causes has discovered one of the best uses of time. Do you give your time away for the good of society? Think about that with clear-sightedness.

6. You can buy or redeem time

Oh yes! Even though you cannot create time, you can buy it. That does not mean you can add more time to your life, but you can make more time available for you to do what you want to do. Let me give you a simple example. Have you ever hired someone to do something for you? Yes, I'm sure you have: your electrician, plumber, gardener, or painter. You paid them to do the work not only because they were skilled, but also because then you didn't have to spend the time doing the work yourself. If you liked, you could have painted your house yourself. You may have had to spend time learning how to paint a house and then more time doing the painting, but you could have done it yourself. But when you hired someone else to do it, then you bought that time for yourself.

Okay, what about when you buy food from a restaurant rather than spending the time cooking it? You spent money but you gained time. That means you can buy time. Anytime you pay to gain time, you have bought time. Similarly, if you have lost time in the past, you may redeem that time by doing something differently now, so you can regain the time. For example, a student with a chemistry exam around the corner might have used a significant amount of time playing video games rather than studying chemistry. Therefore, that student will need to work twice as hard to prepare for the chemistry exam to make up for the time used playing videogames, meaning they need to redeem time. Whether buying or redeeming time, you make more time available to do something else, and what you do with that time is up to you.

Looking at all the ways each of us can control what we do with our minuscule slice of eternity, it is obvious that we must be judicious in our approach to time. We must strive to make that small portion of Forever meaningful and use it for something valuable. Our existence is governed by this law of time, this interruption in Forever. We must open our minds to what this means: it's an opportunity to become a steward of the currency of life, to become accountable for how much time we have each been given.

Time as a Measure of Life

How old are you? That was the question my son, at nine years old, asked a friend of mine immediately after greeting him in the foyer. My friend replied with the number of years he had lived. It occurred to me then that your age *is* your life. The real answer to "How old are you?" is "What and where is your life at this moment?"

The passing of time is the gaining of life. The greater the amount of time you traverse, the greater is your life. Your life is over when you cannot spend more time here, when you run out of the currency of life. Time is a measure of life. The arithmetic difference between when you begin and when you end equals your life, and that can be 1, 2, 3, 10, 40, 50, 100 years or more. Let me now ask you, "What and where is your life?"

You may be wondering what I'm trying to achieve with that question. Seeing your life in terms of time will help you put your existence into proper perspective. We all must first realize that we have lives roughly of the same size. If you live a long time, you'll probably get seventy, eighty, or ninety years. A small fraction of people may get a hundred or more, but we generally live less than a hundred years; this is common to all of humanity. If you think about how much time has passed since the beginning of time, that is minuscule.

That should get you thinking. Your slice of Forever is like a brief flash of light, appearing in a moment and fading away quickly, compared to the entire length of the interruption in Forever. If science has helped us determine the universe has experienced almost 14 billion years of time so far, then how much of that equals your own slice of time? The answer is only about 0.00000067 percent if you live to 100 years. It does seem like we just appear and disappear, with a limited amount of time here on this planet.

You may be curious to know what this all means. It means that you and I do not have forever to do things. We must become conscious of the reality of the brief time we each have. Those who are clear-sighted and see life with their insight understand that time must be managed, and its use must be controlled. Most importantly, everyone must spend time on what really matters to them. Without that consciousness, that insight and perception, many people will reach the end of their lives being frustrated and regretful because of the misfortunes caused by lost opportunities. And these misfortunes simply come from the mismanagement of time. How *long* we live does not matter as much as how *well* we live. How well we live depends on what we do with our time.

Some years ago, around the time I turned thirty-nine, I was reading the story of Dr. Martin Luther King Jr. Dr. King seemed to have done so much with his slice of Forever. At least I thought he did so much. So I decided to see how long it had taken him to accomplish what continues to resonate with all of us more than fifty years after his death. And guess what? That man died at the age of thirty-nine. That was a light-bulb moment for me. Although my slice of eternity is not identical to Dr. King's, I needed to evaluate my journey to be sure I was spending my time on what really matters. Dr. King could have spent those thirty-nine years wasting time, dilly-dallying, moaning about injustice instead of doing something about it, and hoping for longevity. If he had done that, he would never have made the difference he did.

Let the use of your time be in alignment with your assignment in life.

You do not have the whole of Forever to succeed, start a business, enter politics, complete an education, develop your talent, be with your family, excel in your job, or do anything worthwhile. Let the use of your time be in alignment with your assignment in life. Do not let your story be that of someone who spent their slice of Forever and left behind no trace, sign, or mark of their existence. Do not be blind to the true meaning of time. Do not let time elude you because of a lack of insight. Whatever you must do, do it now. Let time, the measure of your life, work for you.

Time as a Successive Trio of Life

One of the greatest tools available to humanity is the existence of time in the form of three consecutive successions. Unlike in Forever, time enables us to live life in pieces and smaller slices. Although the interruption in Forever provided an incredibly large amount of time, we get to live life moment by moment, one slice after another. However, that slice of eternity that you have already lived cannot recur. You can only live in the portion you have in the moment, and you must wait for the slices ahead to arrive.

Time exists as past, present, and future: the trio of life. Yesterday is gone permanently and will not come back again. Today is here and we must live it while we still have it. Today will soon become yesterday. Tomorrow is in the future, and we must look forward to it. Having life divided into past, present, and future makes living easy for us. The trio of life becomes the foundation of planning and change. We can plan because we can divide time; we can separate the current moment from future moments, and we can determine what to do in the future based on what we do today and our past actions.

Here is some good news: the fact that the past cannot come back into our existence means we can always start all over again. For example, you might have failed yesterday, but today that may change. You could have been sick yesterday, but maybe today you are not. Life is unlike it is in Forever, where everything is eternal. If you are poor now, you can plan and work hard to change that. Once you change it, it becomes your past. We can put things in the past. In fact, we can completely do away with the past, bury it behind us. We can disconnect the present from the past. We can put the past in the past and focus on the moment.

Similarly, we can postpone things to the future. One may decide to do tomorrow what they could do today; that's procrastinating. Conversely, sometimes we are unable to achieve something today, but we may try harder and achieve it in the future. The future provides hope. The fact that hope exists is one of the miracles of the interruption in Forever. We can all look forward to something in the future. We can anticipate tomorrow. We can plan for tomorrow. If we do not like our circumstances today, we can decide to change it and make tomorrow better. What a great opportunity!

Meanwhile, what is most important is how we use the present. We do not have any control over how we used the past. It is gone. We also do not have immediate control over the future because it is yet to come. But we have control over the use of today, the current moment. We can change our experience of tomorrow by what we use our time to do today. We can live only in the current moment. In fact, we live only one moment at a time in our slice of Forever.

Those who are clear-sighted do not worry about the past and are not apprehensive of the future. They live in the moment. That too is a perspective; it is all about how you see things. A lack of insight makes one stuck in the past. Forget about both your successes and your failures of the past and focus on what you need to do today. The only guarantee that your life will count for something meaningful is what you do today, in the moment. Every moment that passes is a portion of the currency of your life spent forever.

One more thing. Your entire life and my entire life will soon be in the past. We will eventually run out of the currency of life. The only thing that will remain is the footprint we left as we took our steps in yesterday, so we must carefully take more steps now in the moment. What kind of footprint do you want to leave?

Nothing Is Permanent in Time

I'd like to end this chapter with this nugget: nothing is permanent in time. That may be good news or otherwise, depending on your circumstance. The point is that nothing in the interruption of Forever lasts forever. There is a beginning and an end to everything in Forever's interruption, in time. Whatever begins must end. It is a universal law.

Time as a universal law of life guarantees that there will be an end to anything that begins.

Remember that I mentioned that time is a relief, a break, from Forever. That means if we are in Time, everything must be temporary. The only place where everything is perpetual is in Forever.

If you're going through a tough time or experiencing loss, failure, sickness, disappointment, lack, or any other unpleasant phase now, just remember it cannot last forever. Time as a universal law of life guarantees that there will be an end to anything that begins. Either the situation changes in time, or you run out of time. It will all end. Similarly, no good phase lasts forever. Everything ends.

What should this mean to you and me? No one should hold on to anything in this life as if it will last forever. It all depends on how you see. Some live in hopelessness and despair in this life because of how they see. They see their temporary hardship as permanent and act accordingly. Some see themselves as superior in this world, doing as they please daily, usurping power unto themselves, living large, oppressing others, aborting justice, and becoming law unto themselves. They have forgotten that we will all eventually run out of the currency of life.

Your daily actions reflect your insight or eyesight, your ability to see clearly or your blindness. It is sound judgment and keen insight to act with the understanding that nothing is permanent in time. One operating with clear inner sight within time will embrace fairness and justice, live in freedom, lead a simple but impactful life, accomplish much, and find fulfillment in their work. Everything is temporary.

CHAPTER 5 SUMMARY

I opened this chapter with an abstract description of the perpetuity of Forever and a description of the Grand Master of that domain. The Grand Master decided to create an interruption in Forever. And there it was, the fundamental law of life: Time, the currency of life. How you see and use time determines everything in your life. There are six ways you may use time:

1. You can spend time.
2. You can waste time.
3. You can invest time.
4. You can save time.
5. You can donate or give time away.
6. You can buy or redeem time.

Time is a measure of life, and no one has forever to do anything. Let the use of your time be in alignment with your assignment in life. Do not let your story be that of someone who spent their slice of Forever and left no trace, sign, or mark of their existence. Do not let time elude you because of a lack of insight. Whatever you must do, open your inner eyes, find your path, and do it now.

In time, we live life in pieces, such that we can separate yesterday, today, and tomorrow. We can leave the past in the past and we can plan what is to come. We can separate the current moment from the past and the future.

One operating with clear inner sight within the law of time will embrace fairness and justice, live in freedom, lead a simple but impactful life, accomplish much, and find fulfillment in their work. Everything in time is ephemeral.

Chapter 5 Action Items

Take some time to go over the story at the beginning of this chapter again. Then assess how you see and use time and complete the following action items.

1. Think about the fact that you only have a minuscule slice of eternity, that we do not have forever to do anything. What do you need to start doing immediately with your time? You may need to develop a plan to guide you on the journey through your slice of Forever. You may even need to develop your life's blueprint as I discussed elaborately in my book, *Pursuit of Personal Leadership*, so you may want to use it to help you. Write down what you would like to achieve in your life, your specific actions, and when you will complete those actions.

----

2. How does the fact that everything is temporary shape your perspective about your situation? Are you going through a hard time now? Or are experiencing a mountaintop moment? Whatever the case is, write down a statement that shows your understanding of this concept.

---

3. Think about the footprint you will leave after you run out of the currency of life. For example, list three things you would like to leave behind as your legacies. Then write down the specific actions you will start taking now to work toward creating them.

Taking Off Your Blindfold

Why do you see the way you do? Each of us has an underlying reason we see the world the way we do. Think about an iceberg, whose tip is the only visible piece of it while nine-tenths of its whole volume is submerged. What people do, say, and express is only an indication of what lies beneath. How you view the world reflects what is inside you, how you think, and the content of your subconscious mind.

The way to change how you see is to alter how you think. Remember that *what* you see is a function of your eyesight, but *how* you see is a function of the insight, perception, and judgment of your mind. Throughout this book, I have provided information to help you alter your thought processes and shape your views differently. Do you need to unlearn what you have always believed so you can alter your perspective and begin to see the world clearly? Yes, we all need to continue to learn, unlearn, and relearn.

The crux of this book is for each one of us to learn to become clear-sighted, to start seeing with clear inner sight. We need to start seeing other people clearly, dealing with the self-centeredness that we learned from birth, learning the real meaning of respect, removing biases, building bridges, and being the solution. We must also see ourselves clearly and seek to become our "true self" as discussed in this book.

We learned that each one of us must take self-responsibility for finding opportunities and work hard to grasp fortunes. We can all possess a rich expanse of gold, but we must see clearly enough to spot them. We cannot afford to let either failure or success becloud our view of opportunities. Learn the seven-step recipe for finding your rich expanse of gold as presented in this book and you will find it.

What about the fact that your intrinsic self cannot be tamed despite the systems that might have shaped you? Your ideology and personal philosophies might have been shaped by your environment, religion, social media, and the like. However, if what you imbibed from the systems that shaped you prevents you from seeing clearly, it is still your responsibility to break free from the influences of those systems while still acknowledging them so you can see above and beyond them. That will require you to become open-minded so you can learn differently. We must free ourselves from limiting beliefs and parochialism. We must then become the source of illumination and agents of positive change for the world.

And what do you do when you are at rock bottom, when you get beaten down and you face what looks like the worst situation in your life? The rock-bottom experience requires a change of perspective, a shift from focusing on the problem to seeing the situation in four different ways: knowing that you are not alone, accepting that the only direction to go from rock bottom is up, knowing that no situation lasts forever, and seeing rock bottom as a solid foundation upon which to build an edifice.

I also discussed how each of us lives only within a slice of Forever. Time is the currency of life. You may spend, waste, invest, save, give away, or buy time. Time is a measure of life. Therefore, your use of time must be in alignment with your assignment in life. You cannot afford to allow time to elude you. Do what you must do now. You should also leave the past in the past and live in the present to work toward the future. You should be clear-sighted enough to know that nothing is permanent in time, that everything that begins must end.

Going back to the beginning of this book, we now see that the true definition of blindness is a lack of insight, perception, or judgment. The greatest devastation that anyone can experience is to possess physical sight but lack the clear-sightedness of the mind, to be devoid of the ability to see the world clearly.

The key message of this book is that you need to remove the barriers to clear-sightedness, the dense fog that beclouds people's understanding and prevents them from leading effectively, running successful businesses, accomplishing great things, reaching personal goals, and fulfilling personal visions. I hope you heard that key message.

Remember that I mentioned in this book that nothing changes until you change. Ask yourself what you need to change in you based on what you have learned from this book. Return to the action items at the end of each chapter and act.

What would you do differently from now onward? If a particular part of this book resonates with you, what actions could you take to ensure that you implement the lessons learned?

To achieve the best results, I recommend that you refer to each chapter of this book, absorb the lessons, make the personal change required, and become a better agent of change for society.

I Have a Dream

Let me close on this note: Dr. Martin Luther King Jr. gave his famous speech, *I Have a Dream*, on August 28, 1963, calling for freedom and the abolition of racism in his country. Just like Dr. King, I too have a dream. I dream of a world where people in positions of authority, people in politics, and average people will be willing to rip off their blindfolds, cure their blindness, and deal with the injustice of the racism and prejudice ravaging our world. I dream that nations, communities, and individuals will deal with their neighbors with respect, build bridges, act as connectors for others, and become the solution to the common problems the world faces today.

I dream that the gap between the elite and the common person will close as more people begin to see opportunities clearly using their insight, thus locating their own rich expanse of gold and harnessing the potential that has always been there for every human being to tap into. I dream that everyone who reads this book and those who hear about this book will make a conscious effort to follow the steps for locating their rich expanse of gold as laid out here. I dream that you, the reader, will determine to rid yourself of limiting beliefs or parochial philosophies, reinforce positive beliefs, then dart into the wild to become your true self. I dream that you will continuously—with an open mind, insight, and intuition—break the psychological barriers to thriving in the world.

I dream that anyone at rock bottom who reads this book or learns about this book will find the courage to rise above their limitations. I dream of hope for those who are distressed and of strength for those who are standing. I dream of a better, just, and progressive world as we each traverse our slice of Forever.

Most importantly, I dream of an impactful and fulfilling life for you and for me.

I hope you have been inspired by this book and that you enjoyed every page. I would like to ask you to kindly leave a review or rating wherever you acquired the book or simply go to Amazon, type the book title, and leave a review.

Let us connect.

www.deleola.com | LinkedIn | @TheDeleOla on Twitter & Instagram

About the Author

Dr. Dele Ola is an award-winning author, an accomplished professional engineer, and a change leader with a profound level of experience in corporate circles and a strong voice in the leadership development community. He started his career with Accenture, a global Fortune-500 company, before transitioning into the Canadian polytechnic applied research system.

Dr. Ola is the director of the Technology Access Centre for Aerospace and Manufacturing at Red River College Polytechnic, serving as a major contributor to applied research leadership. He earned his Doctor of Philosophy in mechanical engineering from the University of Manitoba. He has held many leadership positions and served on the board of several prominent organizations.

Dr. Ola's book, *Be A Change Agent: Leadership in a Time of Exponential Change,* won the business category of the 2021 Next Generation Indie Book Awards and has a growing readership around the world. His second successful book, *Pursuit of Personal Leadership: Practical Principles of Personal Achievement,* was released in February 2022.

Dr. Ola is passionate about corporate leadership, personal growth, skills development, and technological innovation. An active leader in innovation and applied research, Dr. Ola continues to lead change in his work and the world. His vision is to develop change agents to challenge the status quo, take charge of the future, and evolve into what they are meant to be in life.

Notes

Seeing Clearly Is Not What You Might Think It Is

1. "Erik Weihenmayer," *Erik Weihenmayer*, 2023, https://erikweihenmayer.com/about-erik/.
2. "Blind," Merriam-Webster Dictionary, last modified February 8, 2023, https://www.merriam-webster.com/dictionary/blindness.

Chapter 1. Changing Your Mental View

1. Doug Dollemore, *Scotch® Transparent Tape*, American Chemical Society, September 19, 2007, https://www.acs.org/content/dam/acsorg/education/whatischemistry/landmarks/scotchtape/scotch-transparent-tape-historical-resource.pdf.
2. Stuart Anderson, "55% Of America's Billion-Dollar Startups Have An Immigrant Founder," *Forbes*, October 25, 2018, https://www.forbes.com/sites/stuartanderson/2018/10/25/55-of-americas-billion-dollar-startups-have-immigrant-founder/?sh=276fce8448ee.

Chapter 2. Finding Your Rich Expanse of Gold

1. Russell H. Conwell, *Acres of Diamonds*, June 29, 2008 [E-Book #368], Last updated November 3, 2016, https://www.gutenberg.org/files/368/368-h/368-h.htm.
2. Samuel H. Williamson, "Seven Ways to Compute the Relative Value of a U.S. Dollar Amount, 1790 to present," *MeasuringWorth,* 2023, https://www.measuringworth.com/calculators/uscompare/.
3. Jeremy Norman's History of Information, "The First Successful Oil Well is Drilled in Titusville," Last updated February 4, 2023, https://www.historyofinformation.com/detail.php?entryid=3061.
4. Hannah Smith, "The Story of Oil in Western Pennsylvania: What, How, and Why?" *Carnegie Museum of Natural History*, May 17, 2021, https://carnegiemnh.org/the-story-of-oil-in-western-pennsylvania/.
5. Conrad N. Hilton Foundation, *The Hilton Legacy: Serving Humanity Worldwide* (Los Angeles, California; Reno, Nevada: Conrad N. Hilton Foundation, 2009).
6. Hilton, "Leading the Way Through Hospitality: A Look at Hilton's 100 Years of Industry Firsts," *Hospitalitynet*, April 18, 2019, https://www.hospitalitynet.org/news/4092958.html.

7. Reed Hastings, "CEO Reed Hastings on how Netflix beat Blockbuster," *Marketplace*, September 8, 2020, https://www.marketplace.org/2020/09/08/ceo-reed-hastings-on-how-netflix-beat-blockbuster/.
8. Minda Zetlin, "Blockbuster Could Have Bought Netflix for $50 Million, but the CEO Thought It Was a Joke," *Inc.*, September 20, 2019, https://www.inc.com/minda-zetlin/netflix-blockbuster-meeting-marc-randolph-reed-hastings-john-antioco.html.

Chapter 3. Darting into the Wild Is Key

1. Katharina Buchholz, "Which countries spend the most time on social media?" *World Economic Forum, Future of Media, Entertainment and Sport,* April 29, 2022, https://www.weforum.org/agenda/2022/04/social-media-internet-connectivity/#:~:text=On%20average%2C%20global%20internet%20users,trends%20differ%20widely%20by%20country.
2. *Nelson Mandela Foundation Archive at the Centre of Memory,* "Christmas message of the Deputy President of the ANC, Nelson Mandela," December 12, 1990, https://atom.nelsonmandela.org/index.php/za-com-mr-s-1127
3. *Nelson Rolihlahla Mandela 18 July 1918–5 December 2013,* "Message by President Nelson Mandela on National Reconciliation Day," December 16, 1995,

http://www.mandela.gov.za/mandela speeches/1995/951216 reconciliation.htm

Chapter 4. Hitting Rock Bottom Is a Good Thing

1. Alex Wheatle, "I felt so alone and rejected—until my prison cellmate taught me about belonging," December 29, 2021, *The Guardian*, https://www.theguardian.com/lifeandstyle/2021/dec/29/i-felt-so-alone-and-rejected-until-my-prison-cellmate-taught-me-about-belonging.

About Dr. Dele Ola's Award-Winning *Be a Change Agent*

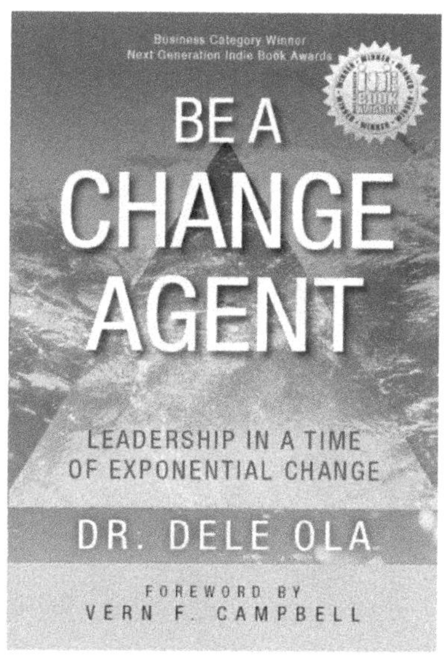

Are you painfully aware of the mismatch between outdated approaches and our rapidly evolving world? Dr. Dele Ola looks unflinchingly at the problem of resisting change and offers a wealth of expert guidance on how to embrace positive growth and foster development.

Be A Change Agent is a comprehensive examination of change leadership: the need for it, the qualities of change leaders, and the importance of having great change teams. Dr. Ola first guides the reader through stories of fearless leaders and explores the Veritas qualities that made them successful. Then he discusses building collaborative teams that work well and have the independence to innovate without overt bureaucratic control. Dr. Ola's years working with high-performance teams helped him develop an insightful tool for looking at three spectrums that cause tension in teams:

- The Systems Spectrum-Structure versus influence
- The Reaction Spectrum-Reflection versus action
- The Perspective Spectrum-Reality versus idealism

And the Tensions Equalizer tool will change how you view the balance of members in your team. Finally, the book culminates in a discussion of the future of work, learning, enterprise, and innovation.

Complete with insightful questionnaires and reflection questions, *Be A Change Agent* offers a practical toolkit for both emerging change agents and seasoned influencers to evaluate their leadership qualities and become the very best they can be.

About Dr. Dele Ola's Pursuit of Personal Leadership

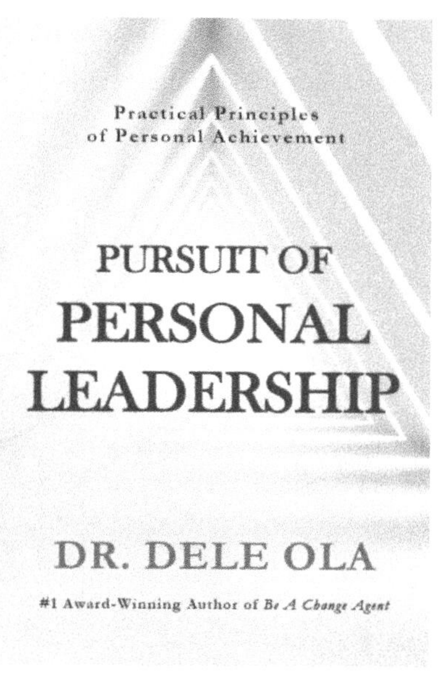

The definition of success and personal achievement is not universal as success comes in different shapes and sizes and at different life stages for everyone. For those looking at where they are and where they want to be and wondering how to get there, do not look any further. Using real-life examples, Dr. Dele Ola presents proven, practicable, and timeless principles to guide you on your journey to great achievements, a journey he calls, "the pursuit of personal leadership."

Dr. Ola has learned that you can only attract great achievements and make great impacts through a process of personal change and imbibing the culture and discipline of successful people. The world must make room for someone who has discovered, and has the desire and determination, to develop and exploit their gifts, talents, and abilities to establish themselves in what they have determined to be their exact purpose and calling in life.

In *Pursuit of Personal Leadership*, Dr. Ola highlights a missing piece in leadership literature, which is the discovery of one's personal identity. He explains the need for a personal blueprint for success and how to develop your blueprint. Learn how to cultivate the necessary personal leadership attitudes, exploit your creativity, discover and establish your life's work, explore the world of possibilities, and understand the five seasons of personal leadership every successful person experiences.

Most importantly, all successful agents of change should understand and embrace the responsibilities of role modeling success and leaving a legacy.